I0475982

Romancing
YOUR *Career*

Romancing YOUR Career

Shabnam Asthana

PARTRIDGE

Copyright © 2017 by Shabnam Asthana.

ISBN: Softcover   978-1-4828-8885-0
             eBook   978-1-4828-8884-3

All rights reserved. No part of this book may be used or reproduced by any means, graphic, electronic, or mechanical, including photocopying, recording, taping or by any information storage retrieval system without the written permission of the author except in the case of brief quotations embodied in critical articles and reviews.

Because of the dynamic nature of the Internet, any web addresses or links contained in this book may have changed since publication and may no longer be valid. The views expressed in this work are solely those of the author and do not necessarily reflect the views of the publisher, and the publisher hereby disclaims any responsibility for them.

Print information available on the last page.

To order additional copies of this book, contact
Partridge India
000 800 10062 62
orders.india@partridgepublishing.com

www.partridgepublishing.com/india

CONTENTS

PROLOGUE

Today I make another addition to my overfull bag of emotions – the emotion of fulfillment! Today I feel fulfilled! Today I also realize that a single emotion can host a set of sub emotions, because *this* is a different kind of fulfillment. In my book **"Romancing Your Career",** I have dropped the carefully cultivated polished exterior of the perfect professional and given you a glimpse of the proverbial "behind the scenes" activities. I feel happy, I feel vindicated, and I feel exuberant.

Thinking of a topic for my first book was for once something easily said and easily done, I guess this ease stems from the fact that it is only people and things close to you that come readily to your mind. The dilemma however, lay in its classification, was my career to be categorized in the former or the latter? Was it animate or was it inanimate?

My career has been as inseparable as life itself. It has permeated my very being with wonderful emotions and enriched me immensely. What ensues in the following chapters is not a natural, linear, mundane progression of my career, but in fact a medley of memories, people and incidents that come randomly in my "mind's eye" as they would for all people who are in love, for love defies chronological orders, dates and sequences.

It redefines importance and relevance when seemingly unimportant things suddenly assume a life determining significance and the routinely important ones are reshuffled in the priority list.

What emerges after you pen your thoughts is a wonderful ballad of memories and experiences which were always latent but have now been brought to the fore to be relived and relished.

I recall, my disappointment when as a child I was not permitted by my parents to attend a school picnic, my adolescent years when despite my best dance steps and moves in a local dance competition I walked home with a consolation prize, or the shock of that incident when I donned crisp starched new clothes with a new bob cut hair style and walked in to a party with my father only to be complimented on what a good looking but a tad skinny son I was. I recall my disappointment after listening to all the rags to riches stories at why I was economically and financially well placed, regretting the absence of a ground zero platform to take off from. "Why was I born in a comfort zone if I had to make it big one day?" I chided myself mentally. My assumption being driven by the common belief that only those born and brought up in the lower echelons of society would work their way up, depravity being highly conducive to breeding success, while those who were reasonably comfortable in life moved on from one comfort to another with ease. They did not need to make great career discoveries and be lauded for those.

The above incidents though, left me with a feeling of incompleteness as if there was something I had to achieve and prove not to the world but to myself. I felt engulfed with a desire to aim for something beyond my line of vision; something which would make me enthralled at its appearance and make me go weak in the knees. I discovered all these and much more in my love – *My Career*.

I could either blame it on the stars or applaud them for it but I admit with vehemence that star power was at its potent best on me. "Leo Traits - Warm, action-oriented and driven by the desire to be loved and admired, Leos have an air of royalty about them. They love to be in the limelight, which is why many of them make a career in the performing arts."

I feel happy, when I am noticed as soon as I enter a room, I feel happier when I continue being noticed even after the initial interactions and am the happiest when I am remembered well past the end of the meeting.

I have evolved from the hesitant yet ambitious lady who entered the world of PR to the mature, confident woman very comfortable in her skin and self worth, a woman who has numerous awards and accolades behind her and has to probably opt for a one size bigger cap to accommodate the growing no of feathers on it. Regretfully though, I am still embroiled in a non conclusive battle of trying to make a few people understand that it is the cap and not the head which has grown in size. I continue in my futile efforts to make them realize that a lot of hard work and toil has gone into making me what I am today, and if I recount an achievement by picking up the phone, or texting it in a social media group, it is only because I am excited to see my efforts fructify, I am excited at being singled out from the clutter for a recognition or an award, I am happy to be considered as a first ever Indian speaker at an International conference and all these should not be bracketed together under the common label of "showing off." It stems from the joy of sharing and it is the happiness of understanding and encouragement which I in turn seek from them. I humbly acknowledge the existence of people moving around with larger caps and realize that I still have a long way to go.

Some have derived great pleasure in probing into the private compartments of my life which I have not yet uncovered (purely because as the word implies they are private and have no relevance to the public,) adding their own conjectures with great conviction and imaginary closeness to me, have termed my positive work related travel, as escapades prefixing it with unpalatable letters of their choice.

I have been alienated by a few close people who believed that if 3, 4 or 5 of them stood together, I as the 4th 5th or 6th, would most definitely feel small and unwanted. I have a special thank you for such people because they have made me realize that the biggest strength in the world and more so in the corporate world is not dependence but self dependence.

My profession has awarded me a unique PHD degree. The uniqueness and difference being that unlike a paper qualification it's a mental degree awarded by yourself, where P stands for passion, H for honesty and D for dedication towards your profession.

The fact that I enjoy dressing up, wearing makeup and keeping abreast of the latest trends in fashion is because I enjoy my feminity and this particular aspect that it embodies. The fact that I sometimes shell out money from my pocket for luxury hotels and first class travel in case the sponsored company trips do not include those, is not to propagate a "holier than thou attitude" (since we still fall in the domain of the working class, entrepreneur or otherwise, and these are deemed avoidable frills and luxuries) or If I can sport a solitaire, or make the best brands a part of my wardrobe and shoe rack, it is because I have a soft spot for luxury and all that is entails but most importantly I feel immensely gratified and happy that I am able to afford it on my own. I am guilty of being proud yes, but this pride has in its bank account my limitless self worth and love almost to the point of insanity for my profession.

Yes, I do get along better with men and have more men friends than women, but it's because I choose friendship over gender and in today's modern world if one is gender rooted in all that they do, the roots are sure to weaken and make everything attached to it topple over.

Your profession is a storehouse of various volatile situations and accompanying emotions, you have to provide the safety switch of maturity and experience to prevent any short circuits. What I write henceforth in the subsequent chapters is heartfelt and first hand. I do not attempt to sermonize or criticize, for how can I be a party to something I myself am averse to? I attempt to take you through some painful, some joyous, some *ooh la la* moments of my career and would be delighted when you recognize a few characters, empathise with them or get inspired by them during the course of your reading journey!

I am greatly indebted to my father **Onkar Nath Panchalar** for the inspiration that he has provided and continues to provide from his golden abode above, to **Deepak, Snigdha & Deb,** who love me for what I am, my darling Labrador **Scooby** for introducing me to that part of my soul which lay undiscovered and without whose love and affection my very existence today would be incomplete and unimaginable and lastly my soul mate, the love of my life my **Career** for teaching me to be **ME.**

As you dear readers turn the pages to begin your reading journey, I turn mine, towards a new tomorrow, pursuing yet another day in my profession with new longing, new expectation and a surfeit of love……..

CHAPTER 1

PROSPECTIVE SUITORS AND THE PERFECT MATCH!

While we regale in the word individuality and strive hard to establish one, our oxymoronic existence gives us inevitable reality shakes at various junctures in our life, leaving us vulnerable and reactive. So, by that logic, individuals while being independent entities are also universal, in terms of the choices that confront them. Then is the choice itself universal or the feelings that are associated with it?

Without delving more into the childhood ones, I do a fast forward and halt at a career choice. I am a staunch disbeliever in the word paucity or deprivation either singularly or in any of its manifestations and firmly believe that life has always been liberal in doling out choices to one and all. In fact, making an intelligent career choice from a plethora of abundant possibilities instead of a dearth of them can indeed be a daunting task. I was no exception then, when it was my turn to embrace one.

A career in my opinion is akin to a suitor; it is something that you have to commit yourself to and therefore has to be given careful consideration. While lending an ear to the oh so many advisors, it is ultimately your head and heart that clinch it. With a great choice of suitors unleashed, I embarked on the expected task of elimination and a possible selection. Taking recourse to my fertile imagination, I did exactly what I had been doing in the past in the wake of multiple choices that I was posed with - the time tested mental cinematography. With this in place, I was etching out various roles for myself - as a doctor walking through hospital corridors, holding on to syringes and scalpels with comfort and ease, or as an airhostess precariously balancing eats and beverages on a tray at 35,000 feet, a teacher inking and writing out my destiny as well as those of my attentive pupils in exercise books and blackboards, then with a dash of glamour it was strong lights, layers of makeup, lights, camera, action, and I was an actor and performer with loads of public adulation. However, all these roles had the common thread of emotions running through them - trepidation to excitement, nervousness to confidence, Yes, I have lived it all in my personal mental span, living and re living them till I zeroed down on one, which fell into the popular choice category. There was something intriguing about changing course from the taught to the teacher wasn't it?

So finally, the garland of hopes was placed around this suitor who held my hand and took me to the classroom and his world of scholarly promises. The scene of action during this period progressed from junior school teaching to High school teaching to teaching in a prestigious Defence Academy. Each experience unique in its own way. It is amazing how you don the cap of the role you play, with such ease and simplicity. Minnie Mouse, Donald Duck, nursery rhymes, tongue twisters were indeed the all consuming reality centric world for me when conversing with the junior souls of my teaching universe while poems of Keats, Byron and Shakespearean plays dominated my universe as a High school teacher. The strong smart spirit of the military academy campus permeated my being and I graduated from a common man or should I say woman, along with the cadets to a world of bravery, camaraderie and the all consuming passion and love for my motherland. I lived and essayed all the roles with a great sense of belonging and enjoyed and reveled in all that it had to offer. Teaching is indeed an enriching experience and it would be apt to say that it's not about what one imparts but what one gains which can neither be tabulated nor chapterised in text books; such in fact, is the wealth of experience and knowledge!

After a courtship of a few years with books for company, timetables and routines, annual exams to serenade with, give advice, see either careers made or hopes of some students dashed, I felt the nudge of impatience and the desire to change course. With this came a fair share of misgivings and doubts about a career choice made after due deliberation and which was meant to last a lifetime much like my precious suitor, but was now giving way to this restlessness. I groped and struggled with new feelings and emotions that were enveloping me, in fact I could sense a strong duo. What was it? Was it the guilt pang of straying, infidelity, the failure to remain committed? But no, wait, there was a stronger one lurking at the back which was akin to exhilaration and an all enveloping ardent desire … yes I did manage to identify it finally, it was the excitement of venturing into the unknown with my intuition as the navigator, spurring me on. It dawned on me that once again my oxymoronic world had unleashed and revealed a new reality – that of permanence itself being transient!

In my mental arena various contenders came forth once again each trying to outwit the other, making my next choice very challenging, but taking recourse to my power of "brain rein" I named the winner. Yes, my next prospective suitor and probably my perfect match would indeed be Mr PR (Public Relations)….. feeling lightheaded, and heady with excitement I realized that my foray into this exciting world with my new suitor had just begun….. this new found choice would see me graduating from guilt pangs and clandestine encounters to a bold and public disclosure of this relationship. Yes my choice was indeed made!

Our career universe is dotted with multiple choices so why should anyone be limited by the first choice which they thought would be everlasting with an air of finality? In fact, a series of decisions will eventually culminate in a final choice, so one should continue experimenting, choosing, yet remembering to give each choice and career relationship their very best and be confident and sure that one day they will finally meet their match which will defy transience and transform their career world into a state of permanence.

"Starvation of your true calling will only breed dissatisfaction but intense desire and timely action will see its' satiation. Remember nobody writes scripts with you in mind, but the clapper board is in your hand - so go ahead, play your part with as many takes and re takes till you can that perfect shot."

CHAPTER 2

FAMILY INTRODUCTIONS...
MEET, LET GO, HOLD,
BEHOLD.......

It is one thing to have the boisterousness of youth, and the recklessness of throwing caution to the winds in following your passion, but for any newbie at a job including me the question that bobbed into the mind was now that we pursued our gut feel how could we continue to make this our dream role?

The first day of my corporate encounter had all the excitement of the proverbial first night. It saw me donning my best and most flattering outfit, I even made a mental note of the colours used in the company logo and attempted to make at least one colour in my clothing match that. I don't know why I did that since logo colour coordination was nowhere mentioned as a measure of success, but the young and reckless me was gripped with the think "out of the box" concept and even carried this to my attire.

As I stepped into the haloed precinct of the reputed Multinational Company, my excitement knew no bounds. After the formal induction and round of introductions when I was being led to my desk by the HR Manager my heart was beating so fast that if there ever was a death by excitement I was about to meet mine, but suddenly with the same intensity that it was racing it came to a screeching halt "Could it, could it really be true?" Started echoing in my mind but halted as suddenly and surely as it had started, as we sped past the imposing looking table and chair that I had set my eyes on and was pointed to a rather non descript corner table. The condescending look that I got from the HR Manager coupled with the unspoken lines of "really, did you seriously even for a minute think that would be your cabin? Well you have to work your way up, look at me I am still not there."

Gradually my corporate life picked up to a fast paced greetings, meetings, presentation routine interspersed with the coffee breaks and lunch times that also served food for thought and grapevine for beverages.

Amidst all this I could feel the first stirring of love, the waiting, the covert glances, the dressing up, the make up, the racing of heart beats whenever I beheld the dark silhouette the inviting aura of - the powerful high backed chair, yes I was head over heels in love with the cabin and all that it entailed. The position, the title and I was unabashedly admitting it, so vocal was I, that when the HR Manager during his routine "make the employees comfortable" internal rounds asked me where I would see myself 5 years from then, I pointed to my love and said 5 years is too long I see myself there earlier.

So while my confidence and love for my job saw me sailing through most part of the initial years I did have my fair share of dampers too. A newcomer is inevitably dismissed with the line "you are new let a few years slip by, then you will know what we want and you will see things differently." "You will be more experienced by then"

"Before you joined us we used to do it like this" and so on and so forth…is what I got to hear on many occasions during a company presentation. The perpetual presumption which I had to battle with was that of experience judged only by the passage of years. I endeavored to impress upon the nay sayers that having the zest to perform perfectly and in tune with company expectations, with enough preparation over and over again was an equal if not better mark of experience. I went all out to meet these wise men and women with a good many years in their age bank with this unspoken conviction and with the "I can do it" sparkle in my eyes. I would not be wrong in proclaiming that this did see me through in seemingly difficult situations.

My career partner's family had doubting Toms, pooh poohing Janes, demure or passive –"It doesn't bother me" cousins, "I told you so" siblings, "I knew it before you" cool dudes, "let's help you" condescending uncles, in fact close encounters of every imaginable kind ! So with so many family members, my early courtship years were the typical enthusiasm meets scepticism kinds, where great bubbling ideas were easily drowned in the hereditary tried and tested work bowl.

Business jargon embodies terms such as - meeting halfway, being receptive and being open minded. I decided to try the trodden path instead of appearing a rebel. While walking along, I experimented with my suggestions and ideas and convinced people to adopt them. What emerged at the end was a wonderful blend of the yesteryear ways infused with new life and vision. This is what one should do if one has to survive in today's competitive scenario, was my wise observation.

Starting with the positive assumption that you are young and new so your ideas will be out of the box and strikingly good or countering it with a negative one that your youth itself will be a disqualification and would rank low in the scale of success really holds no ground as I found out. What should be done is to dispel the notion of being a newcomer and work as a "hands on" professional. Try strategies and ideas, experiment with them for the perfect result and prove your worth.

It helps to be a great observer and start off with a spirit of learning in whatever job you choose to do. I remember during my teaching days I was more of a learner than the learned, imbibing new ideas, the Institutional culture, experimenting, adapting and finally fitting in. This followed in the corporate world as well, as I metamorphosed from the figurative hesitant cautious caterpillar in a home grown orthodox family controlled corporate to the multi hued butterfly in a culturally diverse broad minded no holds barred, Multinational, with independence and freedom complete and backed by flexi timings to work and perform. This is what I carry today, to my entrepreneurial venture as well.

My change of profession contrary to coming as a rude career shock came as a welcome heady experience, with each day donning a new avatar. When you begin your day with the surmise that no two days are alike, you carry it through right till the end of your day packed with the excitement that any novelty brings. This in fact, as I have learnt from experience is the best way to dismiss the pre existing mental monotony of a routine mundane 9 – 5 job.

Excitement, novelty and opportunity lurk at every nook and corner of your profession. Pre empt it by tuning your ears to hear its footsteps even before the knock!

CHAPTER 3

THE QUINTESSENTIAL EVE

With the ongoing, intriguing, endless battle of the sexes, debates & arguments on gender equality which seemingly are endless what then should a working woman's stance be? Well, all the women are working I do not quite buy the "we are just home makers "or "housewives "kind of a description. Housewives and home makers are as much a part of the working class as the working women themselves. The only pronounced difference being one class steps out of the confines of the home and spends their time while the other breed works and spends it within. Now with the modern work from home emergence I believe it's time for a third definition to surface - the working home makers or homing workers the title is yours for the choosing. So when the crown of responsibility was placed on my young head I stepped out to join the breed of working women. My path criss crossed with men at various junctures lending its fair share of experience to recount. When you are young and also endowed with relatively good looks you get noticed. Now, before your mind starts working overtime, let me attempt a clarification, this analogy is like choosing between different colours – black, green, grey, red, yellow the entire rainbow. The colours attract you depending on your choice, this does not necessarily zero down to the superficial clothing and make up but the colours of your personality, your wit and intelligence which believe me are tangibly radiant and appealing even at first glance.

I have derived immense pleasure in getting noticed (and have no hesitation in admitting it.) If you are a presentable woman you have a natural edge of getting more noticed than your other counterparts in any scenario even a female dominated one. At the onset not having known that career and professional roles were indeed gender defined and gradually with this realization seeping in I decided to revel in this advantage (yes I choose to call it an advantage) instead of battling it. The highlights of my teaching days were the oh so many chivalrous men who would hold the door open for me to step in, according courtesies meant only for a queen. Then there were those brash loud ones who made you instantly aware of your feminity, emboldened by the belief that raised volumes would definitely drown the softer ones and get noticed. Surprisingly I learned that there were many of the females who too, practised this art if you could call it one, having picked it up from their male peers. This was something which I was averse too and time and again this thought came to me –why were we taking the liberty of destroying and re designing this original God hour creative masterpiece with our reckless man hour labour? This surely wasn't meant to be so even if you sang Que Sera Sera the future was what the Creator had destined it to be………..

Each woman as much as each man can dismiss and dispel stereotypes to accommodate the new Ms or the new Mr. definition. For instance, when you see the wink and "let's meet after dinner" kind of a look you can counter it with a "No I am not interested" fixed unnerving gaze which believe you me has the potential to repel the most persistent advance.

As a frequent traveller and an International one at that, you probably have more exposure to interaction with the entire gamut that mankind has to offer. I recall an instance when I was a young traveller waiting at the lounge of a busy airport I could sense the alcohol infused "want to catch up? Can I get you a drink?" interested glances coming my way from a well dressed, bored yet adventurous gentleman. Sitting next to me was an elderly female traveller, who was darting pearls of wisdom my way recounting what had happened to attractive young women travelers who chose to wear clothing with high hemlines and how one should be careful as inexperienced as I was with the ways of the devious world where unpalatable things happened under the garb of business travel. I guess, the well dressed bored adventurous gentleman was the cue for her to steer away from the family and work related topics that our conversation was sticking to earlier. A restless and uneasy me found the perfect opportunity to put an end to this when in a no public address announcements business lounge, the staff of the efficient Virgin Atlantic made the announcement of their flight by asking those seated in a loud voice "Virgin? Virgin?" as they inched towards me and asked me in a loud voice I mustered enough vocal power to be able to shout louder than them and say "No not anymore" "Taken"……. Which met with a few shocked expressions, looks of disapproval, or smiles and laughter from those within hearing distance and resulted in two people promptly changing their seats - the well dressed bored looking adventurous gentleman and the wise elderly lady!

This impish urge to outwit and shock people worked well and I spent a few peaceful undisturbed hours before boarding. "It wasn't a double entendre was it?" I said with a chuckle to myself, as I made my way to the boarding gate, it was indeed factually correct because on earlier occasions I had flown Virgin Atlantic but this business trip was indeed taken by British Airways!

Laughter and wit aside, on a more serious and bothersome note I hadn't fared too well in curbing my emotions and feelings when my initial professional successes were pooh poohed with disdain. Taking you back to the tall dark silhouette of the chair in the Head PR's cabin and my all consuming love and intense desire for it saw my derrière on it in less than 2 years. To say I was in the seventh heaven of delight would be an understatement, and my immense happiness knew no bounds, but one man's happiness is another man's hell and true to this saying I had to constantly whisk away words and unflattering adjectives of how I had made my way to that chair probably by being too close and in greater unethical physical proximity with the powers that be, in return for my seat advantage. It was even more perturbing to note that such uncomplimentary verbosity had female origins, and also women who were not a direct part of the corporate itself but were associated as the spouses of the males inside carrying a self acquired commentator status and judging rights of all the women who worked in close proximity with their spouses. Initially, I felt outraged and indignant as I am sure a majority of women too would be, when incredulous looks and "just because she is a woman" are mouthed and insinuated and hurled at you and all your hard work grit, determination, find no place as contributors to the feathers on your cap.

This conjecture became an inseparable part of my career whenever I encountered short quick and early successes in whatever I chose to do and my initial rebellious reaction progressed into a more pronounced calmer approach based on the decision that I would not pander to what the other men or women wanted me to be and operate within a work zone earmarked by them for me. I also refused to join the bandwagon of the gender equality brigade which included an asexual dressing style or the just out of bed look, instead, I resolved to be me and dress up and flatter my feminity, curl my hair, don make up, wear stylish clothes.

By any logical argument where was the definition which said that successful women need to look geeky and unattractive or that successful women need only be well dressed and good looking? I redefined it to suit my spirit, that which allowed me to do everything that I ever wanted to do and go ahead with my hard work, longing and healthy appetite for success.

Success is not gender specific nor does it seek outer appearances to shake hands with, be focused on your work and play your part, either as a natural or all dolled up. Just as it chooses you over another, the designer of your welcome outfit is you and none other!

CHAPTER 4

OF HIGHS AND
LOWS...............

Any relationship is prone to rhythmic movements as opposed to a linear one and the individuals can either play a symphony or create discord through jarring music. When we have a career of our choice we would like to believe that we are creating good memorable music, but is it really so? Do we sometimes have to adjust the out of tune keys, the harsh notes and tone it down to a more melodious one? Yes, we do. When simple things like punctuality, preparedness and good communication go awry for no fault of yours and you are left struggling with deadlocks or negative outcomes, what do you do? I remember many times when I was ready much before the appointed time for an official engagement but my colleague who was to accompany me was delayed and we reached the client's office much later than the scheduled time. I am convinced that even before we made the presentation we were mentally ruled out by them. They had formed the impression that if we did not value the first meeting by coming on time what would we do once they had decided to go ahead with us. In my work ethics I lay tremendous importance on first appearances - first impressions.

It is quite natural for your relationship with your career to go through its ups and downs like any regular love relationship, seeing days of intense love and days of equally intense hatred. I recall getting up early in the morning with great anticipation and longing to go and work and excel in all the intricacies that my job demanded and on certain days get up with a sense of deep frustration and irritation at having to perform the same tasks and as is human nature compare it with other professions and wonder if I would have been better off doing something else. The most heartening thing for me though is that my love always wins over the hate and all things good emerge far stronger than all things bad. The scale always tilts in favour of the good things in my profession. With new developments, technology, the digital age and all things modern seeping in every other day, my profession keeps me on my toes, it keeps me excited, it keeps me active to learn all that the modern world unfurls before us day by day. In my profession and I am sure in a few others as well you can access face book, twitter, instagram and other interesting components of social media as integral to your work. You can travel, visit stores and gain insights into the best of high end designer shopping as an image consultant and get paid for it. You can meet people by travelling the world as part of your PR activity, network to your heart's content and keep adding new dimensions to your career.

What makes me alive and kicking is to get up each day with a new goal and activity in mind. It would not be wrong to say that you can add the zing and zest to your relationship by creating a new spark each day and igniting it with your action. In fact I would strongly recommend PDA's (Public Demonstration of Affection). Talk about your work, tell people how much you enjoy doing what you are doing and that will rub off on you and you will feel each and every word that you say.

I remember a particularly boring day at work when there wasn't much to do and I had to stay till closing hours, so I decided to take out my diary and jot down all the tasks that I would want to do in this profession and which I hadn't really done so far and my list was endless. I experienced a rush of adrenaline while writing out my tasks and realized that the power to dispel my monotony was indeed in my hands. The desire, the planning, the time frame, the deadlines were all so interesting for me.

Discover your career hot spots, and keep it aflame and ignited, dispel the mundane and monotonous by staying in a constant state of intellectual arousal and anticipation....................

CHAPTER 5

BUILDING A NETWORKED UNIVERSE

Any profession demands interaction and since nobody can work in isolation as no man is an island; a saga of relationships is bound to develop. Some as professional as can be, limited to a tight compartment whereas some professional ones gnawing at the boundary wall and seeping in to the personal. I for one am a firm believer in the wealth of networking and relationships.

I remember my first corporate job where I helped an office boy's child with a small loan for the school fees which was promptly paid back to me as soon as his salary was credited and another instance when after office hours, I helped the little child in English before he took his final exam as his parents were from a non English speaking background. It was something very small that I did since I enjoyed teaching and loved little children, but even after having changed my job and leaving that particular company, the office boy never lost touch with me, he would inevitably send me e cards on all occasions and wish me.

It was one of my routine days at work, making client presentations and whizzing in and out of meetings and with the onset of evening came my time to board my flight to Delhi. This particular client that I was visiting believed in a no frills approach so the ticket I got was for the Economy class. I had got quite accustomed to leading a spoilt lifestyle where Business Class was the done thing either when I was paying for it or whether it was the client company, so with a heavy heart I made my way to the check in counter and asked them if any complimentary upgrades were possible. The crew of the airline was in the security check queue right next to me and I could sense their interest in what was transpiring between the check in staff and me. I was given a vehement no by them as there was no provision for complimentary upgrades at that point of time. Resigning myself to the situation and hoping the 2 hours of flying time would pass off as fast as fast can be, I was pleasantly surprised at the boarding gate when my boarding pass was torn and exchanged with another one saying that I had been upgraded to Business class and that too complimentary. Once the initial surprise sank in I started wondering how this had happened. Could it be my assertiveness or my name which I announced loudly to them a couple of times (probably they had a last minute lucky dip and my name came up as a winner?) I was consumed by curiosity but did not want to portray that, so without denting my calm demeanor I managed a "oh thank you, but how did this happen?" although desperate to know what the magic trick was that had worked. However, there was no logical explanation forthcoming from them and with a calmness matching mine they said "It shows in our system and we are just following instructions."

Pleased with my Business Class in flight service just as I was preparing to disembark, I was pleasantly surprised to see the young handsome captain emerging from the cockpit and walking towards me, he wished me and checked if I had had a good flying experience, he thanked me for flying that particular airline. Then very softly he added, "Madam you won't remember me but I am so happy to see you today I am Prateek the son of Praveen Thorat, the office boy in your previous company." It was then that it dawned on me that he was indeed the reason for my last minute complimentary upgrade and I in a small way a reason for his clear, crisp immaculate English "Ladies and gentleman this is your Captain from the flight deck……"

The corporate ladder in my opinion does not read footfalls nor does it restrict people by allowing access to its rungs only to a select few. This truth dawned on me in a poignant moment when after a few years of a gradual climb to success or sprinting across a jungle gym to success as my critics would call it, one fine day at work it was my turn to conduct the final round of interviews for a Senior Management vacancy. Not having had the time to sift through the resumes earlier with a hectic and demanding time schedule, I took a back seat trying to do my homework and go through them there, while the HR Head was conducting the preliminary rounds. I took over the second and final round with my routine questioning. It was then that I heard a familiar voice, a style of speaking, which immediately brought back memories of my boss in one of the companies that I had worked for earlier. Not being able to control my curiosity I peeped in and saw that what I had heard was indeed correct and the applicant was none other than my previous boss! When he walked in to me for his final round I got up and greeted him and accorded all the courtesies that one would accord to a senior and an erstwhile boss of a reputed company. The anomaly of the situation struck me. The courtesies were the same, the respect was the same but a strong corporate gust had ruffled a few chairs and placed them differently.

I must admit that my final decision was indeed a little lopsided with emotions heavily weighted in his favour. I recalled all the encouragement and support that he had once given me and coupled with his knowledge and expertise the job was his for the asking. This gave me an opportunity to practice what I have great belief in which was that as you climb up the ladder, when you look down, remember to acknowledge all the rungs that made it possible for you to do so.

Personal relationships too evolve and change acquiring different dimensions in a working person's life; here I will dwell on what I have perceived from my womanly lens. Pre marriage I had only my parents to contend with in expressing my desire to be a career woman and that met with no resistance since my mother and sisters were pursuing careers too. Post marriage my in laws were of the opinion that a woman should concentrate on her house and rearing up a family however, those were not really detrimental rigid arguments and toppled over in no time. It was smooth sailing till one was just employed and earning the regular decent salary, walking in and out of the work place at set timings. It was when the promotions came in quick succession and the irregularity in timings became the new dictate of the job, that eyebrows were raised and ridiculous, untrue and sarcastic assumptions made. Along with this came the rude distancing from the family sibling circle with shades of green dominating our bond. Whoever coined the term sibling rivalry had much wisdom!

Life is a mish mash of relationships on both the personal and professional fronts, when people look at successful powerful women what strikes them is a bed of roses, it's only a few who recognize what lurks beneath the surface. The steel magnolias have a soft inner core which comes at a price. Leading from the front is not easy as we have to take tough calls, which don't necessarily endear us to one and all, but then we will have it no other way. We do not believe in compromises or things half done. Sometimes women have to wield power in the work place and situations which restrict it or decree female submission. They have to learn to contend with misogyny, criticism and disdain at their creativity.

The workplace and our life is a repository of relationships we have to master the art of sifting and selecting the gems, chiseling and polishing some to a shine and discarding those that are not even worth a dime. We learn how to go ahead and nurture those that add a sparkle and gleam and leave behind the ones that can never be a part of our life and corporate dream!

CHAPTER 6

CHAINS AND FETTERS - STRESS PREVENTS YOU FROM BEING A GO GETTER!

If I were to enter a few popular oft used keywords in the corporate dictionary, I would start with stress. With an interesting lineage, its origins can be traced to both the higher echelons of society right to the lower ones. All of us have been its loyal subject and it has reigned supreme for many years with no end to its term in sight. It has become so deeply ingrained in our metabolism and daily existence that we are hesitant to question its supremacy and its powerful omnipresence. So is it a fad or does it truly exist?

Based on my experience I am inclined to say that it has become a very convenient and easy excuse for non performance. I stepped into my mental time machine and recalled the disheveled hair, messy appearance for official meets, slipping away of deadlines, lost deals, incomplete work, missed flights, absenteeism and the one common reason attributed to all these by those concerned? Well yes, you guessed it right, it was indeed stress.

A Manager in one of the manufacturing companies that I worked for was teamed up with me for a company out station tour to a client company and for making a sales presentation. With the boarding card held firmly in my hand at the boarding gate, I tried to convince myself that he would come and I should not panic. Later with 50 unanswered calls to his number, eyes that hurt because of looking intently at the airport entry, and a tightly clasped boarding card in hand I made my way to the aircraft and looked at the empty seat next to me which would I realized remain unoccupied. Mr. Manager had not only made the company lose money on a no show ticket but this no show would impact me a great deal. My mind started ticking overtime as to how I would meet the clients without him and without having his part of the presentation since the next flight would only be a day later. My cell phone beeped with many messages from him as soon as I landed all apologizing profusely saying he had overslept since he was awake the entire night making the presentation and was very stressed and tense. It was his mental stress which had caused this fiasco was his stance.

Another common occurrence in any failed scenario which never ceases to amuse me is personal stress of the employee which slowly creeps in to the professional space as the individual explains and throws up his or her hands with an air of resignation. Well, spouses, parents, siblings although not physically present have this floating spirit like quality to pull strings and remotely influence the outcome of our work if we have had negative interactions with them.

There are things which seem to be easier said than done but through regular usage prove to be a career goldmine. I attempt to name a few here. You could start off by trying to demarcate your life into different compartments and the compartments must be watertight so that they leave no scope for any seepage to the other ones.

I would strongly advocate the use of stress busters. There can be no one stress buster just as you experience different situations so should you evolve different actions to assuage and cope with them. To name a few - music, popular sport, any hobby, and the wonderful world of pets are some of the highly effective and time tested ones.

My Four Legged Stress Buster - Scooby

The power of music has always worked wonders for me. I for one was one of those who went delirious with joy at the revival of the FM age, driving to and fro from work with my ears tuned in to music in the car, helped transport me beyond the cacophonous world of screeching brakes, blaring horns, loud shouts and yells by angry motorists to a mental world of calm and peace. A word of caution here though, this can only happen if you have somebody else driving you, else you could well be the subject of the shouts and yells of angry motorists and your tranquility could easily become a reality with an easy premature entry to the heavenly abode with its all prevailing calm.

When you talk of practical experience, I claim to be practically experienced in using the power of music beyond words and notes to give my life a rhythm, the rhythm of purpose. There are days when you get up with a not so good feeling about the day and work and although you can lay a finger on the cause of your anxiety, most of the times you can't, it is then when I start the day with music and don't ask me what kind of music. It could be anything from spiritual soft music to Bollywood to Western to rock and roll to jazz to anything that I can lay my hands on and tune in to. This power has to be experienced and the outcome experienced and felt. I term it tangible positivity. Thereon, you emerge a changed and transformed person with a new zeal and desire to move through the day with more ease and optimism. With modern gadgets the power of music is portable. It can be with you everywhere. It can walk with you, it can drive with you, it can run with you and even sleep with you. Music has the immense power to permeate your being and add melody and rhythm to your world.

Human emotions undergo a sea change and are as unpredictable as the crests and troughs prevalent in the movement of a wave. Who else could illustrate this better than the one I was holding close to me feeling his warmth and deriving great comfort from his sharp fast paced breathing, I was basking in his love, safely cocooned in a territory demarcated by a plentitude of love within. He opened his eyes and I looked at the immense adulation that they reflected. Just 3 years back when I first set sight on him he was a small 45 day old pup brought lovingly by my aunt for me. Not being able to voice my reservations in affections for a dog I had no option but to accept her gift gracefully. Life took a hectic turn thereafter with poo and pee all over the house and the arduous task of cleaning it. Gnawing of furniture, slippers, clothing was the done thing with very frequent trips to the vet, necessitated due to frequent stomach upsets and vomiting. I would very rarely touch him and even when I did, they would be with gloved hands, as time went by my keen observation opened up a world of goodness that this little being whom we named Scooby embodied. A world untouched by hatred, pretence, selfishness, and intense love for all the family members. He I would say is my biggest solace and stress buster. A pet and especially a dog can introduce you to a pretence free real world where there are no inhibitions.

Yoga, chatting with friends and of course social media are some of the other ones to take recourse to in stressful situations.

I have learnt from experience that stress is self manufactured and marketed to the outside world by us. We are the creators and we are its busters.

Stress is self imposed – attempt to break free!
Stress and Success both begin and end with an S. it is for you to rearrange the alphabets in between and create the word for your personal and professional dictionary!

CHAPTER 7

WHEN BRAINS MEET BRAWN AND WEATHER MANY A STORM

W it, sharpness and intellect are the pre requisites for your visa to the workplace. Paper qualifications alone, stand no ground and are easily blown away by strong winds of brain power.

At the start of my career, one of my responsibilities was to introduce new advertising agencies to the corporate and assign work to them in consultation with my superiors. One such instance that I recall is that of me arranging presentations of 6 agencies including the big, medium and small ones for a presentation in front of the Chairman on his invitation. On the day of the presentation the Chairman suddenly decided to play his superior part to the hilt (because as an insider I knew that there was no hard pressing need for absence) by backing out of the meeting and designating the HOD instead to take a call. Having travelled from all corners of India, they had no other choice but to make the presentation without the Chairman's presence. When the last presentation was left, the presenter loudly announced that he would not present. Walking up to the podium he announced that he was disappointed that the person who had invited them was not interested in seeing what they had prepared. Although his agency fell in the category of the small ones, he spoke with confidence and conviction about what he felt was not done – the absence of the Chairman despite being present in office on that day. The silence that met his words thereafter was deafening – he said he chose to leave the meeting room and walk up to wherever the Chairman's office was to make the presentation. A few muttered words of how busy the Chairman was etc etc by the HOD were met with his "never mind I will wait till he is free." The reasoning that he gave my senior was that he had taken time off to travel for a meeting from Delhi at the invite of the Chairman so if he could fly for 2 hours and prepare for a meeting that was planned a month in advance, surely the Chairman could walk a few steps and honour his invite. Persistence and logic won in the face of illogical hierarchy and brawn power. This incident made me realize that no matter what the size of your organization is, no matter the small medium or big tag that your company has, a man or woman is as big or as small as he / she projects himself / herself to be. The projection of course, has to translate into meaningful action to lend it credibility. The presenter who represented a small company was big by his actions and admission and the Chairman needless to say although big in position proved to be small in work ethics.

Corporate bullying is another aspect that touches every individual in the work force at one point or another. This interesting form is not all about muscle power; it manifests itself in various dimensions right from mental to physical harassment. A demure Ms Joshi comes to my mind as I remember the burly gentleman who used to plonk himself right next to her in the staff canteen loading her plate with dollops of his unwanted food ignoring her feeble attempts to resist and sitting with her right through, till the last morsel was washed down her throat with a large gulp of water. Then Veer who used to hum tunes into his colleagues' ears and distract Santosh from carrying on with his routine work which led to him being pulled up by his superior and being asked to stay back after office hours to complete his task. I have seen some corporate members being afflicted by this deadly syndrome called "steal the thunder." Work done by others was proudly claimed to be theirs and so were the incentives linked to it. Opposed to these obvious easily spotted ones there are a few who work on the sly and with such ease that they would never be on your list of suspects. They work by accessing your mails, your cell phones, all your personal chits / notes and using them to their advantage. Their motive is either to contribute to the corporate grapevine or to gain a more serious advantage like passing on the information to competition, or copying data and using it for commercial purposes, in fact the list of the negative things these wrong doers could do with these is limitless, creating newer and newer possibilities for them each day.

Quick thinking and a high self worth are the two big resources which should be roped together and which you can hold on to, to pull yourself out of the well of negativity.

CHAPTER 8

BOOSTER SHOTS FOR MONOTONY

Midway during my corporate tenure with a decent designation and comfortable take home package during one of the routine days I remember walking to my colleague Linda's cabin; I caught her by surprise which resulted in her hasty rather clumsy action of trying to push something under her chair. Trying not to be too inquisitive was a difficult task as I was engulfed with a deep desire to take a peek under the chair. While our conversations centered on the office tasks and other apparently innocuous niceties, the centre of attraction for both of us was indeed the underbelly of the chair. Seeing no other approach in sight I did what I do best- ask. I asked Linda that I happened to notice her shove something down the chair and if it was nothing too personal I would like to see what it was. A few hesitant looks later she agreed to show me what it was and what I saw was a beautiful sketch of my office colleagues not caricatures but lifelike sketches. I was so impressed with mine that I could not resist asking her if I could take it along and the large hearted girl readily agreed. This set me thinking here I was on a routine day at work experiencing lull and dull periods, with my mind playing havoc unearthing prospects of a job change or other likely scenarios to counteract that and here was this girl one of the oldest employees of the company obviously dispelling these occasional spells of dull periods by doing something that would temporarily distract her and increase her productivity by infusing her with a zeal to tackle the routine tasks at hand after a short indulgent spell. All of us I am sure have a hidden talent under our corporate personality dying to surface and raise its head, so why not keep your outer exterior alive and kicking by allowing your interior second talent to surface once in a while? It will take away the monotony and boredom of a routine job and as for using corporate working hours for honing skills other than what you are hired for let us look at it from another viewpoint, would the organization have a dissatisfied unproductive you warming the chair for 8 hours and a mere physical presence or you at his / her best not staring into space not indulging in gossip but breaking the spells of monotony by providing some space for "Me Time" and productive work thereafter. I am positive they would settle for the latter.

"Stay alive, stay active – discover your hidden talent and allow it to rear its head in the corporate environment not to distract you from work but to infuse you with the zeal to work better."

CHAPTER 9

THE PERENNIAL WELL OF CONVICTION AND BELIEF.....

Most of the synonyms that I can recall make a rather derogatory attribution to the power of imagination or undermine it, for example "yes you can have it in your dreams" or you can only dream about these things they don't exist for real "or" get out of your dream world and face reality." "It's a harsh world out there, be practical don't be a dreamer and don't live in your own little bubble." Enough to shake out the dreamer in you and fling him or her far away to Neverland, but my serenade with my career companion started with the power of imagination didn't it? It prompted me to begin my journey with him and carry it through all the milestones that I had imagined I would meet during the course of our association, so then, why was imagination wrong?

Sitting on the cold iron chair in a queue of prospective bidders for an assignment, my nerves played havoc with me, and my mind was in a state of turmoil, it was only my imagination that unleashed a vision of me shaking hands with the Managing Director after the closure of the deal. This fun play in my mind made me survive the long wait and when it was time for me, it was almost as if I was ready for the win, since I had rehearsed it a million times over in my mind and was ready to meet success. Realistically speaking though, since we have to win real time and not virtually or imaginatively the success rate is much higher if you imagine your victory or success – it works! Well on the flip side on occasions that it doesn't it's still okay, remember you won it in your mind? So there could be a degree of consolation in that.

When you imagine success, it manifests itself strongly and the brilliance of your desire engulfs all those who come in contact with you and then they too work along with you for its achievement.

My foray into the corporate world has driven this truth firmly in my mind that one needs to be realistic and rooted in the physical world but must unchain the mind and let it soar high. The power of imagination is unparalleled and nothing can be more fulfilling than mentally living your success prior to everything that you do.

Being a Christopher Columbus at heart, travel and that too business travel intrigued me no end. The business trip to New York for a crucial business meeting therefore on the 20th of December was a welcome one for me. This time though it wasn't the regular business trip, there was a twist of uncertainty in the travel plan itself. Originally we were a team of 4 people who had to attend the meeting but 3 backed out keeping in mind the weather uncertainties, except me with my heightened state of optimism, devotion to honouring a commitment and restlessness to reach a conclusion which propelled me to carry on with the engagement and travel as planned.

As a well informed traveller with easy access to flight updates and the latest happenings in the world I was aware that flights from Heathrow to New York were affected adversely with unpredictable delays due to weather conditions, so it came as a welcome surprise to me that my New York bound flight was only marginally delayed since I was expecting a longer one. With the long haul flight coming to an end, lighted seat belt signs as well as the captains announcement signalling our descent and landing it was a little unnerving to see that the flight was nowhere near landing despite the landing gear in place, in fact it was an unusually long hovering that was taking place and then suddenly without warning it gained altitude rapidly. Looking out of the window gave us no clue as to the reason since a cloud of white covered all the windows. New York was experiencing heavy snowfall. As I felt my optimism diminish with a strange sense of helplessness enveloping me my mind went back to the other 3 sitting in the quiet comfort of their homes with a "I told you so" "what a waste" kind of a line ready to welcome me on my return. But something inside me refused to give up it was a foolhardy approach though as some would say, with no control on the inclement weather or the joystick, but I had this well of hope inside me which was still full, refusing to dry up. As expected, it was announced that we would be unable to land so would have to unfortunately head back to ......before the destination was announced the PA system was switched off. Chaos in all the cabins, cabin crew trying their best to quieten the cacophony when suddenly the PA System crackled back to life and and and and the announcement that came in drew loud cheers and claps, we were in fact going to land at JFK airport. Bracing ourselves for a bumpy landing our hearts thumping loudly the soft thud of the aircraft as it landed was much lesser than the turmoil in our hearts and minds. Finally I was there, first hurdle crossed. The immigration staff told us that we were the only flight that had landed that day and all others had been rescheduled, which was no mean achievement, considering the very busy air traffic at JFK.

On exiting the airport my eyes widened with shock as the only colour that I could see was white everything covered in white with fresh snowfall continuing unabated. Where would I find a cab how would I reach my hotel in Manhattan was my lingering thought. Taking care not to slip or fall, I made my way to the sign which read "Taxis". Nothing in sight and no one in sight. Clinging on to my stroller which had acquired a new coating of white on its original bright red, dusting away snow from my eyelids and eyelashes I looked around for any moving object in sight. I finally saw a lone man making his way to the taxi stand and standing beside me. Before we could even start a conversation we saw a taxi coming towards us, almost delirious with excitement before I could gather my wits to speak to the cabbie the other gentleman shouted out "Morristown buddy?" the window rolled down just a fraction of an inch and the cabbie shouted out "Nope not there….. Anybody for Manhattan???" Had I heard right? I could not believe my luck could this really be true? I asked myself, as I jumped into the warm interior of the cab. I witnessed huge pile ups of vehicles on the road, with the live skidding of a car just ahead of us… the traffic adventure played on my already distraught nerves and I had to pinch myself time and again to wake up and take in this real life Bond movie action with my cabbie as the central character. I also realized with a start that I could either live to see a blockbuster ending or a flop show with an unhappy ending. I mustered all my strength and prayed for the former. I hadn't flown a long haul flight to have such a short quick ending had I? God chose to listen to me and my cabbie's skills proved to be better than I could imagine and I was finally in the porch of my hotel. The bell boy and the other staff were completely thrown aback to see a guest making her way in such challenging conditions. The door opened and my first impression of the hotel lobby was from cheek level, yes I had made a skidding entry. Ice can be deceptive. After a few consoling looks and tch tch ing from onlookers I managed to shake off the layer of icing on myself and complete the check in formalities. Famished and hungry from the day's adventures I headed to the coffee shop only to be greeted by a bold lettered sign – CLOSED. Even 5 star hotels need supplies as was explained to me and the provision vans could not make it in this heavy snowfall but room service with limited items on the menu was indeed available. Showered and changed I now set myself to tackling the business on hand. A few numbers dialled, initial surprise at my landing from across seven seas for the scheduled meeting crystallized into a formal agenda and course of action. I would be picked up the next day, subject to delays and go ahead with the meeting at the client's office. My preparation for the meeting and more so my enthusiasm with a never say die attitude and oodles of luck I guess led to a favorable outcome and successful closure. It was time for celebration as we headed to the lone, open coffee shop tucked away in an alley; snow freshly shovelled away, ready and welcoming to guests, doing brisk business. I smiled to myself as I sipped my coffee, for someone associated with this coffee shop seemed to be as determined and enthusiastic as me!

The strong anchor of your enthusiasm and determination coupled with Lady Luck has the power to weather all storms and blow away odds and uncertainties. Lady luck however is choosy and greets only those who take the first few steps and cross the initial hurdles to meet it.

Optimism and determination are the stepping stones to success and the bigger the stones the nearer your success!

CHAPTER 10

BE GAZE READY BE GAZE STEADY.......

M oving up the corporate ladder is also inching close to the eye of the storm. With protective covers and blankets yanked away from you, you are left exposed and vulnerable. Picture this- when you were a newbie you could always seek consolation in numbers, namely the number of people who were ahead of you to take on the repercussions of any actions either by you or others in the team including their own, simply because they held a seniority tag to themselves. Accountability and seniority are undoubtedly partners by default.

But as you move up the ladder you are constantly telling yourself to be prepared for such eventualities but needless to mention here that this is easier said than done. I remember a meeting where I had worked really hard on a presentation only to be told later on that my presentation was not even in the running for consideration as whatever I had presented based on the research and company history which another junior colleague had looked into were grossly outdated and misinterpreted. Period. No room for finger pointing, the buck stopped at me.

Be gaze ready Be Gaze Steady

The cynosure of all eyes bit does not limit itself within the corporate walls. If you are at a social gathering or at any other informal event with your workforce you will see this surface more often than not. After a long day at work the evening party did not particularly enthuse me but being a firm believer in the merits of socializing I dragged my exhausted frame after donning it with bright colours and my face with artful make up that took away the monotony and tiredness of the day. A few drinks down and accessories of calmer nerves, smiles and happiness adorned my evening gown. I noticed a few steely glances and hushed whispers from a certain section of the fairer sex. I saw Mrs Gupta making her way towards me and I immediately stretched out my hand to greet her but my hand met a cold blast of air as she preferred to nod her head. "Well well, somebody sure has a magnetic appeal today were the words she mouthed." This was a revelation of sorts because I had never in the world imagined that the homely looking soft spoken Mrs Gupta would make such a stinging remark in public. Her choice of words as I realized was not far removed from reality, my red designer gown was indeed proving to be a magnet for most of the men including Mr Gupta! Wit and sarcasm sometimes do evolve from the most unexpected quarters.

Reaching the top echelons does leave you vulnerable to dissection and conjecture, it's a public life out there with no room for ostrich head sand burials, but in the modern self centred world it is no mean feat to occupy small or large spaces in people's conversations.

When people talk about you, you've made a difference! Accommodate this in your stride by being gaze ready and not letting this blur your vision of the goal that you have chalked out for yourself by being gaze steady! In your line of work watch and prepare to be watched.

Chapter 11

The Elixir of youth

Ever heard the term youth booster? No insinuations, no double entendres here, just making a reference to the pure, unadulterated power of youth. When you are armed with youth, everything around you assumes its colour and aura. The advice and suggestions doled out to you, your receptiveness, your brashness to speak your mind and get accepted, your decision to do what you think best all become a part of the young you. Your moods your lifestyles all converge at the mountain peak of youth.

Many years ago when a young me wandered into the corporate world the Heads of companies were the wise salt and pepper haired men who had witnessed the rising of many suns and moons. As part of my job responsibilities during my initial days I was handling the HR activities along with my PR ones which made me responsible for appraisals, promotions and employee welfare activities as well. Mr. Joshi a short, grey haired gentleman in the Finance team kept pushing his candidature for a promotion only because he had served many years in the organization. With no out of the way achievement to back this claim his appraisal did not conclude with a promotion. It took me a while along with the other senior members of the HR team to make him understand the merit of the work aspect for a promotion consideration rather than only "the been many years around" argument. I did not blame him though since this stemmed from the fact that all occupying senior positions in that particular company were from the senior age bracket.

This worked sometimes to my chagrin and sometimes to my advantage, for whenever we as young people made suggestions they were either vetoed out on the basis of the "do you know more than us kind of an argument?" "Look we are veterans and know what will work and what will not" to "okay this is a fresh new perspective let's try it out!"

When the relationship with your career is in its youthful, exploratory phase, failure is an accepted part along with the excitement and enthusiasm as natural corollaries. During your voyage of discovery you can take risks be bold and do what you please.

There are many occasions in life which embody a spirit of celebration not only for you but for all those who know about it. Birthdays being the most popular one. In my first job with an all pervading enthusiasm and desire not restricted to my job alone saw me venting it out on employee birthdays. In the part HR role that I was doing, I relooked at the traditional birthday cake cutting ceremony at 4 pm. In a bid to make the employees feel more special, I made an attempt to discover all the employees with a talent for music or dance or any other special skills and create a popular half an hour surprise do, along with the cake cutting. This idea at first drew some disapproval from the other team members but then eventually got accepted and became the done thing for birthday celebrations. The slice of cake now had oodles of fun as the icing. Talk of adding a youthful zing to the staid corporate scenario!

Maturity and progression into adulthood comes with its standard set of rules. You are invited to participate in meaningful discussions impacting the policies of the company, the number of years you have clocked in coupled with experience are taken heed of and people look up to you for advise and suggestions. You cannot afford to be brash and hasty, all your actions have to be well thought of and evaluated, keeping the outcomes in mind. You start feeling responsible and answerable and live your role to the fullest.

I remember as I progressed in years I also progressed as a much sought after confidante and was considered the ideal candidate for holding on to personal and work secrets. People started trusting me more as a mature human being. Trust was welcome but the idea of aging did not particularly appeal to me. My mind was active in fact over active and agile and physically I did not look my age so why did my personal and professional world have to be shrouded with maturity and here I infer to only the maturity in terms of the number of years. Was it the need of the hour that I had to behave in a certain way just because people wanted me to behave that way? Everything related to work too became dominated by a maturer perspective. The world comes down a bit harshly on you if you attempt to deviate from the norms and traditions laid out for middle aged people. The thought of fitting into the mould and creating a new identity for myself that was compatible with my age was unpalatable to me, why should I give up the crisp short well tailored skirts and other outfits for formal wear or why could I not don the bohemian flowery flowing dresses that I absolutely loved? Why did I have to underplay my dressing style or my speaking style just because I had gained in years? I felt the same powerful surge of my youthful brashness taking over the middle aged me at that time and I decided to live life on my own terms. I wanted to continue to dress the way I wanted to and speak and conduct myself the way I felt comfortable with, "after all it was my life and not that of the others wasn't it?" I reasoned out with myself.

I was absolutely delighted to see how people accept you the way you would like to be accepted by them. I would not be lying if I told you that at that stage I probably felt younger than when I was 20.

My next job affirmed the shift in the corporate age number game. As I entered the MD's office for my interview a perfect example of the evolution in the age bracket met my eyes. The young smart good looking boy on the MD's chair, who interviewed me and signed my appointment letter, was 30 years younger to me. The time for gauging success and failure in any organization by the age criteria is well past and evolution is the new reality. Rules have been re defined.

If age is a number, choose, define and own yours!

CHAPTER 12

SOLITARY CONFINEMENT - YOUR WINDOW TO SELF DEVELOPMENT

When the recipe of your success is inked out in bold letters and a sequence of events lead to its conclusion, the heady cocktail comes with a formidable mix of solitude and anxiety.

We live in interesting times, the tribe of achievers is increasing by the day and we women are adding our bit to it. Exploring new worlds and new horizons treading paths where no one has ever ventured before. Awards and recognitions came my way, as I made a mark for myself and wielded power in certain sections of societies that limit female creativity and stigmatize their leadership.

The same peers who used to sit with me during lunch time and share the tiffins now walked past with a hasty nod of the head in my direction. Well, considering the scheme of things however liberal the corporate atmosphere is with the current hype on flat organizations, the compulsions of hierarchy and job responsibilities come with inherent rings of distance which forbid proximity. The choice for this rests in your love of the chair. Propelled by your personal desire you may either choose to have a high chair reserved exclusively for you replete with the adorning of power and position or you could choose a chair sans all these frills. Not debating on the pros and cons of either, I would say that if the power to choose rests with you, the power to make the choice work also rests with you. When I chose to occupy my power chair, I could sense many other significant changes. Whereas the peers, colleagues and other workplace oriented changes were the need of the hour or should we say mandatory accommodations, what I failed to understand was the iceberg approach of some near and dear ones. Degrees of comparison are most welcome as long as it spurs you on but not when it harms your well being and corrodes away the root, the foundation itself. For those of you who are blessed with families and friends that rejoice at your successes that should indeed be your most cherished possession for this I discovered is a rarity!

The power of your vision sometimes comes with a personal cost attached to it. While you revel and rejoice with words like steel magnolia, invincible. power woman getting attributed to you, all successful people will vouch for the fact that there lurks a darker shade of grey below the apparent surface of the bed of roses. They are required to take tough calls, lead from the front which doesn't necessarily endear them to one and all. I was no exception. Seeing some of my close relationships slip by in the wake of my new found success I knew that I had the power of choice yet again. To choose whether to mope about my present situation or use it for further advancement.

I opted for the tongue in cheek sibling approach here where words like inner resources, self dependence, inner strength come to the fore to your rescue when you feel your position and power have alienated you and seen the death of a few relationships. Your climb to the top has also seen a more adept you at handling people and relationships as well as your time. The wiser you draws on inner resources, new found calmness, a heightened sense of responsibility and accountability to deal with the new situation. You discover that ownership and accountability are siblings of success which you cannot afford to alienate.

Social gatherings proved to be a useful testing ground. When you are partying with your guard down you tend to enjoy the gathering without any pre conceptions of positions or job responsibilities and it is there that you can sift the sycophants from the genuine people so go ahead and cultivate those friendships. Once you have created a certain rapport with the few, ensure that it stays that way irrespective of the situation or your work pressures, devote the necessary time and energy to hone it.

The other things that cost you nothing yet leave you with a sense of wonder are developing the talents that you may have like singing, dancing, creative writing you name it, the world is your oyster ....

This process of discovery is in fact so exhilarating that you are infused with a new zeal to live life to its fullest. The time pressures of life rarely give a person "me time" so grab it with both hands the moment you see its possibility. Togetherness need not be limited to the human form alone, your partner for a happy co existence can also be your talent, your faith your passion, that come with an inherent fluidity that is more adaptable and you as the creator can chisel and shape and give it the form you wish to.

Contrary to popular belief it is not lonely at the top; you can revel in your solitude, give it wings and create a takeoff pad for a new found togetherness!

CHAPTER 13

CONFIDENCE IS AS CONFIDENCE DOES

The word confidence undoubtedly has a magical appeal which all of us would like to partake in. Its charm is everlasting and leaves all who come in its contact craving for more. There are two profound observations that I would like to make, the first being that confidence grows with usage (etymologically speaking - use and age combined) and secondly a confident beginning ensures a confident ending.

When you are a gawky new comer in the professional world your lack of confidence precedes your appearances at public meetings and only in the rarest of rare cases can you become a true actor who can successfully conceal it by dabbing on a layer of confidence.

Hastily set up meetings, badly planned events, rushed actions all create the perfect backdrop for failure unless you can beckon confidence to tide over it. Confidence as a subject neither features in the school curriculum nor do you have a graduation ceremony for it. In fact this can be home grown as long as you make a beginning by sowing the seeds in your personality.

My senior colleague Raman had reached a comfortable corporate position by dint of hard work and a fair measure of ambition. Being educated at a local vernacular medium school, English communication was definitely not his strong point. In a particular social gathering with guests from foreign shores and a couple of drinks down, carrying and continuing the conversation in his grammatically wrong English he still managed to create an interactive conversation and the evening moved on pleasantly. It was time to wind up and say our goodbyes, Raman excited and enthusiastic with the exchange of words and his ability to make himself understood was suddenly overtaken by ambition to attempt more complicated phrases and words which he unabashedly did, and then came the blooper in retort to something needing him to draw a parallel - "Yes, Yes we are all sailing in the **same shoes**" I was as much taken aback as the guests, but surprisingly the air of confidence which came with the statement that was made deterred us from bracketing it in the blooper category it was promptly dismissed and buried in the exchange of words that continued thereafter with an unfazed Raman. Confidence does come to the confident is what I concluded here.

All of us must have experienced the all too familiar butterflies in the stomach sensation before crucial meetings, events, presentations, you name it. The only tried and tested antidote is to wear the mantle of confidence and move about your business with confidence albeit a false one, this really works wonders as you move and feel your part and work towards becoming a confident you. Since you cannot judge a book only by its cover do take the time to document this by creating supporting pages that would validate and justify your claim to confidence.

Confidence is home grown and you are its' gardener!

CHAPTER 14

BLAME IT ON OTHERS

Non performance, under performance, negligence, and failure co exist in the work culture and so does the blame and the finger pointing game. Blame it on others is a hereditary malady that grows as a second skin on employees. If you are late to work just because you stretched the safe time too much, or took a congested route, were held up in traffic, or partied too hard and woke up too late or you were not prepared for a presentation or meeting because it was not in your priority list or you clean forgot, or you were so busy on your cell phone gossiping that you could not complete an assignment given by the end of the day, the one excuse that pops up is always blame it on others and believe you me there is never a dearth of names that you can think of. If it's not an animate object you always have technology, car, bike breakdown, alarm not ringing in fact the world of excuses is filled with inanimate objects to fall back on.

Mr Gupta was a disheveled perpetual latecomer for anything official. All advance notifications, telephonic reminders, sarcastic comments, reprimands failed to do their bit. It was always blame it on the weather, the traffic, the driver, etc etc. Well he wasn't the only one we had more of his tribe. Mr Bansal, our HR Head after a thorough study of absenteeism and late coming came up with a very ingenious scheme of countering this habit by trying to create workplace pride, self worth and employee bonding, the modus operandi being one surprise a month for chosen employees in which he would include surprise parties, dinners, gifts or felicitation of any family members of theirs who had achieved something noteworthy. Mr Dutta's daughter for example, who became a commercial woman pilot was invited and a dinner held in honour of her achievement, a closely guarded secret from her father and all the employees. In one such event in April we were all invited, and all of us assembled but were told we could not start till Mr. Gupta joined us so after a good one hour of just sipping endless rounds of cola and nibbling on snacks the object of our wait walked in and before we could open our mouths to welcome him he opened his to tell us how his son had met with an accident and had to be rushed to hospital etc etc after concerned glances and good wishes to be passed on to Atul his son for a speedy recovery all eyes turned to the dais and all ears were tuned to the PA System through which the HR Head announced the reason for that day's celebration. Lo and behold what did we have? It was to felicitate Atul, Mr Gupta's son for winning the Annual art competition where the children of all employees could participate. As Atul took centre stage accepting the award amidst claps and cheers one voice and cheer was missing – Mr Gupta's!

Ownership must be in totality, if it is our achievements, our victories, our successes why should we transfer the ownership of everything that goes wrong to somebody else why can't it be our failure our shortcomings, our mistakes?

Ownership and accountability are siblings of success.

CHAPTER 15

CORPORATE BLINKERS

An indispensable, invisible accessory of the corporate wardrobe is a set of blinkers, except that it does not come along as a perk with your appointment letter you have to earn it during the course of your corporate tenure.

Ever wondered how people with different perspectives and different work ethics co exist harmoniously? Well it's because a few of them have mastered the art of turning a blind eye wonderfully well.

Budding office romances, late comings, incomplete assignments due to a lack of ownership covered under layers of excuses, corporate bullying, and sarcasm all necessitate the use of blinkers.

Sheila and Mr Dawson unfortunately did not have recourse to great histrionic skills so it became increasingly difficult for them to control their new found togetherness and liking for each other. It was no small surprise then, that departmental meetings always had a receptionist overseeing the arrangements; in fact Sheila was a permanent fixture in everything that spelled official, and created opportunities for their togetherness. All the other employees took it in their stride and gradually and dutifully we all wore our blinkers.

Then there is the marvellous petty cash and voucher bit where you know that the claims being made by certain employees listing out various customer visits and the fuel charges for those were only figments of their imagination. Rahul for one started his day at the office and the "in between" so called client meetings and office work were all conducted within the realms of his imagination, the reality being either movie time, friend time or family time. So either you play a cop trying to catch the errant guys and become a synonym for all that is right, tread on people's toes and be in a constant state of war, or you opt for the relatively easier option and slip on the eye accessory.

Then there are certain colours that are very popular with the top management, purple and blue being the top picks. Apart from symbolizing the love of royalty and power and position, you have the blue eyed boys and girls who live in a perpetual forced harmony with all the employees since anything said against them would attract the ire of the boss.

"An all encompassing vision assumes a sharper focus when you are blinkered and concentrating only on the objects in your line of vision."

CHAPTER 16

THE SOUND OF MUSIC

Any relationship can strike chords and create a distinct music. A corporate career relationship is no exception. Incidents and events create harmonious streams for you to sail through on certain days or there are waterfalls and torrents of disappointment and remorse on others.

There is no sweeter music than success; I recall a certain incident when I became by default the backbone of a corporate event since the main organizer had fallen ill very close to the date of the event. As a person who was always in the sidelines accompanying the main organizer everywhere I became the popular choice to see it through since I was aware of all the intricacies.

The leader in me took over making it a memorable and flawless event and it was then that my other skills were noticed. I was complimented on my Public speaking, my sense of dressing, my personality, my cross cultural communication since it involved activities between Indians and foreign nationals and of course my complete involvement and "hands on" experience.

It is always nice to thank people for the behind the scenes support but those behind the scenes people must make an attempt to come out from the shadows and be in the spotlight at some point in their career span. I would strongly advocate that being an achiever is one thing but communicating about it is another. If you have done something noticeable and achievable let people know about it. Silence does not take you long distances in your career.

Don't hesitate to blow your trumpet and play the sweet music of success, everybody welcomes good music as long as the notes are not discordant, loud and jarring!

CHAPTER 17

DEFINING YOUR RELATIONSHIP

I f I told you that fluidity has a rigidity and stringent borders have a malleability it would not be a misleading statement, because that is the kind of adaptability that is needed to survive in the corporate world.

You come in with your individual work style, your ethics, your perspectives but they have to soak in the light of other viewpoints and emerge with a palatable outcome. You on the other hand although flexible would still have your limits to the "bending backwards" approach.

Each relationship is unique and cannot be generalized or grouped in the same compartment. Sameer and I hit it off as happy, go lucky, carefree witty colleagues the day we met. His deadpan expression and a whacky sense of humor helped us sail through gruelling situations and dull corporate hours with ease. His work style matched mine and we worked very well together as a team. After a few years of association though, I noticed that the a certain aspect of Sameer's personality, that of being "too full of beans" which had attracted me initially, dwindled into a jumpy, "always on the edge" temperament with a pronounced persecution complex which began telling on our relationship. His Sherlock Holmes bent of mind started getting more and more pronounced. Every word that any of the other employees uttered was for a reason and had to be against him. I tried to reason out with him but to no avail. Gradually we drifted apart and so much so that he was convinced that I too was a part of the charade and games that were being played against him. I could see his blatant misuse of the office cars and cash being diverted for his personal expenses. I along with a few others opposed this and stood up for all that we felt was wrong. This unfortunately made him vindictive and he spared no opportunity to malign and slander us in any way possible. Eventually with too many employees against him he did what we thought was the best way out. He quit!

Then there was the quiet unassuming Radha who hardly spoke 5 words in a day besides the necessary ones that her work demanded and it was she who rushed to hospital when our colleague Vinay met with an accident, she was the first to volunteer financial assistance to him and his family and always stood by anybody who needed standing by in hours of official or personal crisis. Although we parted ways long back when I changed my company yet she remains a permanent fixture on my friends list as I am sure she does in the others as well nobody ever wanting to block or "unfriend" her.

These relationships made me ponder on the words fleeting and lasting which are so much a part of the corporate relationship dictionary.

Be prepared to accept new dimensions and adapt to the ever evolving ever changing corporate relationships.

CHAPTER 18

BEYOND YOUR REALMS....

Transporting yourself to faraway lands and distances with the help of your inbuilt God gifted time machine is a fascinating tool. You don't need a wordsmith to weave tales for you or travel agents to work out expensive itineraries for you. It is truly amazing how a magazine or a letter or an idea can work wonders and that too in the most unconventional surroundings like your office cabin.

Sitting on my chair looking at the various mails and faxes coming in from overseas created fodder for my fertile imagination, as I mentally documented the journey of the little piece of paper transferring hands before reaching its final destination. So this then, became my secret official game as addictive as angry birds or criminal case of the modern days. It's a wonder how you tend to infuse life into inanimate objects through the power of imagination. Every little piece of paper, every magazine, every packet that is delivered to you has its own story to tell. You begin to appreciate its purpose and assist it.

The all too familiar ring came to my ears followed by the familiar sound of paper. Yes it was my fax machine which delivered a document by fax. I could read the itinerary of a Director intending to travel from Sweden to India for a Board meeting. The secretary had worked very hard and the flight details, hotels etc were meticulously planned. A tiny scrawl at the bottom of the document would have missed an untrained eye but it caught mine since I prided myself on having a keen eye for details. At first it was a little difficult to decipher since top designations do not demand good handwritings as a criteria. After executing whatever was mentioned in the official fax and framing and sending a suitable reply, my eyes wandered to the scrawl at the bottom of the document and I could read Taj Mahal and Qutub Minar almost quite clearly now. Resorting to my mental play once again I imagined the efficient secretary typing out the itinerary, and taking it to her boss the Director for approval before faxing it. The Director who apparently was visiting India for the first time had done his bit of reading or speaking to his contacts and noted down those two landmarks which rank very high as India's tourist attractions.

His efficient secretary though carrying out her duty to perfection in ensuring the smooth execution of his travel plans had knowingly or unknowingly overlooked the exploratory traveller in her boss and his touristic yearning. Sometimes you are in a quandary not knowing if what you are reading in between the lines is what is meant to be and whether you should tread beyond the call of duty to grey zones not demarcated for you. However, being a little adventurous I did my own research on the two tourist spots, guided tours, prices, air connectivity, in line with his travel plans and compiled the information and sent it to the Director marking a copy to his secretary. A little restless not knowing how this little initiative would be received at the other end; I went about my routine tasks. After a day, the familiar sound of the fax machine churned out a letter marked to me. It was a letter that complimented me on the work that I had done and also requested me to finalise the tours as per the information I had provided. Enthused by this response I went about doing so with great zeal.

The realm of your job is dynamic and borderless with infinite possibilities; it would be futile to attempt a demarcation!

CHAPTER 19

DUMB CHARADES

G ames that people play are a familiar song for the corporate ear. At some point of time all of us are familiar with this popular corporate game either as judges or participants.

It is a boon to have a superior who doesn't take the superiority aspect of the designation to cloud his dealings with his subordinates. Alex was one such boss I had, who as all of us jokingly said left the Head of Department as a fixture for the name plate on his door. He was in fact a buddy, all ears for our suggestions, problems, in fact with us through thick and thin. Working for him was a pleasure, and it wasn't surprising then that everybody wanted to put in their best and his department was always the star performer in the corporate pageant.

Close to the end of the financial year, everybody in his department including me was given tasks that required us to put in many work hours and also do a lot of research and paper work. As was the rule for all work delegated by him we had to store all the information and data in his personal computer and not keep any copies of it even for ourselves. Not only this we were told not to discuss our findings and reports with each other as well keeping the confidentiality of this project in mind. We had to make numerous visits to our company's go down and store where all past history and files were kept to dig out long forgotten information as well and hand it over to Alex for compiling in his report. With the team spirit and enthusiasm at an all time high working for a boss like Alex who interspersed our arduous hours with lavish treats (of course at company expense) that included lunches and dinners at 5 star luxury hotels with liberal alcohol for those who wanted it. March end saw our findings ready and delivered to Alex. I distinctly remember that 31st March was a Sunday that year but none of us exhibited even an iota of resistance in sacrificing our family time or holiday and working for Alex on that day. The end of the day saw us enveloped with a sense of satisfaction on meeting our deadline and also being showered with words of praise for our sincere and hard work by Alex. After all we had worked for our buddy and not our boss.

As we all breezed in to office the next day on the 1st of April expecting the usual warm greeting from Alex, we were surprised to see his cabin door still locked. This came as a big surprise to us because punctuality was his biggest virtue and in case he was being held up with some work or was intending to come in later than usual, one of us would definitely receive a call or text from him telling us so. Yes he had followed this practice for at least the 2 years that I had been working for him. I must admit that there was a fleeting conjecture by a few to the linkage of the date 1st April (April Fool's Day) and the absence of Alex but it was cursorily dismissed as a majority of us were convinced that he was neither a teenager, with a frivolous work approach or a prankster.

No information about his whereabouts even two days later and his office and personal phone switched off we decided to visit his house and check. Another surprise awaited us as we saw his bachelor pad locked and bolted. Enquiries with the security guard and neighbors yielded no results either. Nobody had seen him of late and had no idea where he could be. Our concern and the HR Head's routine check on uninformed absenteeism took us to the Managing Director and then began a proper investigation by digging up his records his parents contact numbers and so on. Mr. Kamat the HR assigned a representative for the job. A week ended with unanswered queries and ongoing investigation. 14 days later we were summoned to the Managing Directors cabin. The mood inside was somber and we somehow with a sinking heart feared the worst. We the team of 8 nicknamed by our other colleagues as Alex's angels who had worked so hard for him and the assignment he had given to us were bracing ourselves to hear something which definitely was not good news as our instinct told us.

And then we heard this….. We were told that Alex had joined competition. The entire two months we had been assisting him in gathering information through market research and our own company records in compiling a project report for a start up and entrant in the same segment as ours. Alex had joined as the CEO of that company with a massive salary hike and perks. He had in fact misused the company and his staff for furthering his career and ambition. Shell shocked and with moist eyes, weak in spirit, we made our way out of the MDs cabin and we felt ourselves floundering in this uncertain world where hope and trust are obliterated from the corporate dictionary when it is placed in the hands of people like Alex.

The corporate sports field houses and introduces us to many games but the outcome of it with its winners and losers remains elusive and unpredictable!

CHAPTER 20

OPTIMISM IN THE FACE OF HURT AND DEJECTION

An inferiority complex I was told when I was in school creates bullies. I could not have agreed more as I saw this unfold in the daily corporate drama of one of the companies that I worked for. Manager Shriram as he was called was short, dark complexioned and middle aged. I do not cite his physical appearance by way of a disqualification or demerit but only because it will help you imagine how he appeared. Manager Shriram had served 15 long years in the company and the comfort of his chair was something that he was ardently devoted to safeguarding. Coming from a vernacular background and rather elementary education, he was always on the defensive at meetings and public gatherings where he I am sure felt his vulnerable best. Then one fine day we had a new entrant - Ragini - a tall beautiful confident girl. As she walked into Manager Shriram's office he saw the word threat and insecurity occupy a hitherto empty space next to his precious chair. This sincere, smart and young, girl as he grudgingly admitted to himself with her resume in hand was much better qualified than him. Manager Shriram had made an urgent request for a junior in his department considering the work pressures and tasks on hand and while he was on a 20 day sick leave recuperating from a minor surgery, the MD and the HR Head had conducted rounds of interviews and appointed Ragini. Feeling sidelined at not having had a say in the selection, Manager Sriram alias MS already had his animosity unleashed. Round of introductions over, work explained the enthusiastic girl set about her tasks. It was for all to see the no opportunities spared for humiliation rounds that started coming Raginis' way. She being a soft spoken girl and a new entrant was hesitant to retort for fear of ruffling a few feathers. That I believe was her biggest mistake for nothing encourages bullies more than acceptance of their bullying. MS would make derogatory remarks on her sense of dressing and style. The corporate had a morning tea meeting where Asst Manager and above grade of employees would all assemble in the pantry and over tea, discuss any departmental interactions that needed attention or any work which was pending and so on, the idea being that roadblocks could be removed in a social and amicable way instead of circulars and memos floating around. As we all assembled for one morning meeting the door opened and Ragini walked in to take a seat too. A loud guffaw of laughter and all heads turned towards MS "Ragini your leave is granted for today." flustered Ragini looked around and asked "Why Sir?" "Well with the kind of makeup and clothes you are wearing surely you were heading to the beauty pageant being held at the 5 star luxury hotel next door, isn't it? You would surely be welcomed there, okay leave granted ...." And then more laughter. Nobody present including me commented on this sarcastic remark and the meeting continued, with MS gloating in his little victory of embarrassing Ragini. Gradually MS intensified his attention on Ragini, no no, don't get me wrong here it was more as a butt of ridicule and favourite nit picking object for him. Ragini took this in her stride but we caught glimpses of her moist eyes and blushed cheeks on a few occasions.

Welcoming each day with a smile

The sudden passing away of the Chairman of the company saw the second generation take over the reigns of the company. When the old order changes new concepts, new work styles, new decisions tend to follow and this company too was no exception. There were the golden handshakes, summary dismissals, re structuring of departments and so on. There is a light at the end of a tunnel they say and the spotlight shone on Ragini, as she took over as the Manager of her department, a discretionary, out of turn promotion given by the New Management. Strange are the ways of the corporate world – the man MS had walked in through the entrance door that morning but by evening the man who was walking out was RMS – Retired Manager Shriram.

Perseverance and optimism - blind bullying and pessimism with their brilliance!

CHAPTER 21

ALL WEATHER PROOF

The corporate entry point has no security check and you are permitted to bring in your woollens, coolants, umbrellas in fact all that is needed to protect yourself from the onslaught of unfavorable weather within.

The unique aspect of the corporate saga is that although it does not create a chapter by chapter narration for you, it still gives you the opportunities to co author it by infusing it with your words and spirit and taking it to the conclusion you want.

The herd mentality rules the corporate wisdom with employees unwilling to make any deviations from the accepted norms and practices. Contributions for birthdays, weddings etc are the one thing with everybody following suit. As a new employee with a thin take home packet the 700 employees strong team had some occasion almost every day for which we were all expected to dole out a minimum of 100 Rs. This understandably, started making a big hole in our pockets. Grudgingly, unwittingly, the employees still continued the practice. I established a first of sorts by belling the cat and saying it should be voluntary and not mandatory to do so. I was surprised to see my move garner the support of a majority of consents till finally the practice shed its mandatory aspect. This small change then paved the way for many other small and big changes and it was a welcome re look time at the old policies and traditions.

Picnics and social gatherings are a much looked forward to event if they are understood in their right perspective. A social gathering is not the arena for satiating the urges of starved corporate Romeos with casual apparently accidental brushing past or jumping up to greet their women colleagues with a hug or the oh so so long lingering handshake. When it rains unwanted affection the women need to open their umbrella of protective cover, be it the company of an understanding colleague male or female, be it a strong hands off body language message or a polite "I am not available" kind of look. The dress code chosen by your female colleagues is in all probability the party code and the "because I want to dress up kind of clothes," short skirts, high hemlines, deep necks, netted and lacy garments are not transmitters for sending out signals, so dear Casanovas please don't attempt to interpret nonexistent Morse codes or SOS. Please go easy on those rising testosterone levels, there are a million other productive (pun intended) ways to vent it out.

The corporate cycle of seasons has its spell of summer and heat when you face the wrath of your seniors for something wrong either intentional or unintentional that you may have done. This is when your inbuilt air bag for absorbing the intensity of the impact is called for. Ire with ire, a volley of words in exchange for another volley, noise for noise is definitely not the answer. Patience, resilience, calmness are all the positive attributes that work wonders during a corporate tiff, show down or dressing down. The one at the giving end is often reflected in a poor light if the receiver reflects it and counters it with a stoic response. If both parties are in a bid to outdo each other and there are occasions when you will either exhibit or witness amazing lung power, (which also provides a false sense of victory to the participants) then of course it becomes the preview of a show without any tickets to attend providing much fodder for gossip later.

Relationships with your peers, your seniors your juniors also have a freeze angle where all that is exchanged in between are the cold vibes and glassy looks, relationships where once the ice was broken and thawed has returned to its original state – frozen !

There may have been many reasons, many angles which resulted in the existing cold state. You again have to take recourse to your mental and emotional machinery and find a "thaw way out" for those that matter and are integral to creating a conducive work atmosphere. When we are at our intuitive best we use our coping mechanisms carefully and prudently to increase the balance, focus, and awareness in our careers.

Your corporate years are influenced by a change of seasons; you have to gear up to be a man or woman for all seasons!

CHAPTER 22

PRETENCE AND BEYOND

All of us, well let me change it to most of us at one point of time or the other are guilty of using this extremely seductive tool to further our career advantage. We pretend to be more knowledgeable than we are, we pretend to be more informed than we are, we pretend to be more overworked and stressed than we are, we pretend to be more well travelled more better off in every which way than we are.

There is much truth in the saying that "it's better to keep your mouth shut and be called a fool than to open it and remove all doubts." Sagar a living example of pretentiousness was lucky enough to get past difficult and tricky situations except for this one. It was the day of the Board meeting and also a coveted chance for creating a good promotion impression in front of the Directors and other Senior Management. His presentation was impressive and body language just perfect to grab eyeballs. Then came the tricky part where the number game was unleashed and quick calculations had to be made for future plans. One of the Directors suggested taking the help of a calculator and also a Finance guy to aid Sagar in his effort, however, that was promptly declined by him saying he was a wizard with numbers. The meeting started and Sagar in his sitting posture would take only nano seconds to come up with computations and results of complex calculations. All it took was a pensive expression and a downward glance to mull over for a second and then spring up the answer. The proceedings were nearing a close when the last computation met with a long silence from Sagar. The Board members tried to cheer him on and asked him to come up with the final figures which unfortunately worked no wonders. Sagar's downward glance grew more downcast and eventually resulted in a fist thumping show down and a show of great impatience as he finally stood up and threw away his watch. Well that then was the treasure chest of all his promptness. The million dollar question that popped in everybody's mind at that time was how one pretence can obliterate all your hard work and show you in poor light. Conceding that it wasn't a major crime that he had committed it still did its bit to erode the carefully crafted impression of a deserving and smart employee that he had succeeded in portraying earlier.

Pretence is seductive - use it with caution, playing with fire is an art where only a skilful few come out unscathed!

CHAPTER 23

THE LAW OF ATTRACTION

Every relationship, every situation every occurrence embodies an element of magnetism, albeit in varying degrees. I have always vouched for the fact that the more attracted you are to a cause and its outcome or conclusion, more chances of you succeeding come into play.

Swadesh the Man Friday of one of the companies that I worked for was very ambitious. He wanted to make it big in life. As he would tell everybody he wanted to add 2 more zeros to his salary of 9000 Rs to make it 9 lacs. This fancy figure and the thought of achieving it kept him on his toes as a willing student. He had a goal but no supporting plan. With nobody from his family being able to understand his desire to excel and achieve more and not having anybody in his family to talk about this, he zeroed down on me to express his heightened desire for more money and success.

Occasional conversation exchanges between us during lunch breaks or other free time saw me pepping him up and encouraging him to improve his communication skills. I could see great enthusiasm in his eyes whenever he spoke about augmenting his income and status and discussed various ways and means by which he could do it. I, as a well wisher would add my bit to it. After I quit that company to join another one I lost touch with Swadesh.

Standing at a traffic light waiting for it to turn yellow, my eyes turned towards my right and then lo and behold I could not resist my urge to call out loudly "Swadesh Swadesh." For it was indeed him in a 4 wheeler. We got out of our cars and he asked me to join him for coffee at a leading 5 star hotel nearby. This change and progress although very welcome was also a little difficult to digest and I could not conceal my surprised wide eyed look. Swadesh's next step took me completely by surprise, he conversed only in English. As I walked towards him, I complimented him on his achievements and also asked him to give me an insight on his progress. With a sense of pride and happiness written large over his face he informed us that the overtime compensation he had got and was getting had made him earmark a certain amount for English speaking classes in his area and he had gone ahead with a year long module. He had also joined computer classes so that he could be of some assistance in case needed.

He had taken a conscious decision along with his wife and children that he would make a new career move to supplement his income.

The efforts and determination from his end had seen him move very close to the add zeroes mission. It is true that the more you imagine yourself achieving something the more you attract it.

The second aspect of this attraction is in fact very literal. The attraction between the sexes. The coexistence of males and females in the same office space does fan this attraction as well as the complications that come with it. You have typical Bollywood workplace romances, some not so serious and some so serious that it ends at the altar.

Subramanium was a character who was cast in a very different mould; nothing about him exuded happiness or enthusiasm. Every day he would report to work imagining the worst that could happen to him or his work. So potent was his negativity that it would inevitably rub off on whoever came in close contact with him. Every job that was delegated to him would die a sudden death even before he started working on it. So positive was he about the negative outcome. He killed his enthusiasm and that of the others as well. It was a part of his job responsibility to set up the Meeting rooms with the requisite stationary and audio visual support. For an important meeting one day he went through the regular drill of checks and re checks for this gathering was for 120 people from different companies. Everything was in place whoever was assigned the different tasks catering, anchoring, presentations etc was well rehearsed and prepared, but in walked Subramanium with is doleful expression announcing loudly that he was convinced something would go wrong despite all the efforts. This sentence was enough to dampen the enthusiasm of all present there but they shook it off and went about their tasks diligently. It was time to start the programme, the anchoring, introduction all went off very smoothly. Then came presentation time and then began Subramaniums' struggle the projector just would not start. The Emcee tried to buy time by interspersing some last minute add ons and talk but yet nothing happened. It was shameful and a big letdown for our company as this technical glitch was just not acceptable, Subramanium looked at me and muttered in an undertone "I told you so I was sure something would go wrong," Rohit the presenter was however endowed with a positive mindset and ventured to say that he was not dependant on the projection of the presentation and had everything in his mind since he was the one who had prepared it and a whiteboard and marker were enough for him to carry on. We called for some assistance to shift away the tables and make space for a white board and marker. The thin boy who was attempting to shift the tables broke into loud laughter and suddenly stopped since realization dawned on him that it was a public corporate meeting and laughing so loud was definitely not deemed acceptable behavior. As most of us looked quizzically in his direction he signaled to Subramanium with his hand and moved his finger slightly and then voila the projector came on...... what had happened we all asked? "Oh nothing Sir forgot to switch the power button." So caught up in his world of anxiety and negativity was Subramanium that he kept attending to the complex chords and wires and gadgets to ensure that they were in working condition so focused was he on the complex that he overlooked the simplest.

Attraction and Imagination are interlinked we attract what we imagine. A small positive thought, a small positive step is all it takes to counteract the negative, slowly but steadily!

CHAPTER 24

REFLECTED GLORY

A widespread corporate epidemic which affects Secretaries, HOD's, HR people and some other species of employees is the **"busy syndrome."** This is particularly infectious and goes to the head and other body parts rapidly inflicting them with the deadly virus of self importance. This malady though remains self limited and is not contagious or passed on to their superiors. They take great pride in being the carriers of this deadly virus and make no attempts to vaccinate or inoculate themselves.

The first category mentioned above is the most affected. Whenever you call for their bosses the well rehearsed standard line of "he is in a meeting" greets your ears. When after a couple of calls they run out of this line they switch over to "he is travelling" and moreover they make you believe that even they don't know when the boss will be back because his / her plans change as they have to accommodate sudden meetings in their busy schedule. Oh, then how do they cope with their ticketing etc do they get last minute seats? I wondered. "Well the airlines know him well so he enjoys a privilege status you know and so on and so forth" Wasn't I glad I didn't work for an airline where I would have to keep certain seats empty just in case a Mr. so and so would drop in anytime? "Nevertheless, I must admit that the excuses and reasoning get better and better by the day. They never ever run out of excuses to ensure that you never get that desired appointment and if you luckily do, then it would be after a long wait and an arduous drill of several phone calls, emails, messages, texts and extensive follow up rounds.

The HR fraternity on the other hand suffers from meetinggitis. Perpetual rounds of job interviews, training exercises, employment letters and various other documentation keeps them from meeting outsiders as they are very very actively engaged.

My words of wisdom as a PR professional would be that the first point of contact for any individual be it the secretary or the HR executive is a million dollar opportunity for a good impression. Dear secretaries I know you do a difficult job but let those messages those phone calls reach your boss instead of being just a strong thick filter, try not to soak in too much power from the top source, limit it to your role and designation. Let me let you into a small secret; I sported this designation for a year too and understand that this is not an easy seat to occupy.

HR people we love you but we also know that you can't be in meetings all day. Give each caller, each visitor his due if he deserves attention give him an audience, if he doesn't tell him so politely. Your juniors can do so only to a limited extent; it is for them to inform you and for you to decide the future course of action. You have to have work to be busy and that is very acceptable, but just using it as a word to keep visitors and callers at bay, will be diagnosed as the virus of a disease that breeds in your designation, by the modern well informed outsider.

Your accessibility and importance should neither be curtailed nor overplayed by others. Certain corporate roles are not meant to be just filters to sieve appointments or sponges to soak and bask in reflected glory!

CHAPTER 25

APPEARANCE MATTERS

I am tempted to contradict the proverbial saying "Don't judge a book by its cover" As a PR person I would say, a good cover is the indicator of good content. We, the working class are a hypocritical lot when it comes to the dress code. On days when you are in a tearing hurry and unable to give much attention to your clothes and appearance you feign the "I am a serious no nonsense person in terms of dressing or it is my work that will take me places and not my dressing style." On days that you have shopped or have new clothes or you sport a new hairstyle which you would like people to notice, the reason that you give them for your deviance from your usual norm of dressing is that it was either your anniversary or some family occasion and so on. You wouldn't risk saying it was your birthday because that falls in the public knowledge domain and somebody could call your bluff.

Sonia was by nature a laid back cool person and not very dressy at work. Her choice of clothes was ruled more by convenience than by adherence to any fashion or style. In fact when she was in a group she would never stand out in terms of clothes or personality. She would so easily blend in the group with no individuality

Nikita, on the other hand was always abreast of the latest fashion trends and looks, be it clothes, haircuts, accessories for work and so on. Since both of them were a part of the CRM team comparisons were bound to happen. Both of them had their share of brickbats and bouquets from their colleagues with some in favor of the fashionista look of Nikita and others for the Plain Jane look of Sonia.

At events and social occasions it was always Nikita who was given the role of hostess or any jobs that involved coordination with the public and guests, nobody specifically mentioned why but yes all of us could understand that it had to do with her presentable personality and appearance. I would even venture to say that people acquire the personality of the clothes they wear. If you are clad in simple and functional clothes for work you tend to present yourself as a workaholic, a person who is very down to earth and whose only focus is work and nothing but work. On the other hand the person who spends considerable time dressing up for work (by dressing up I don't mean heavy makeup or designer clothes, it means anybody who gives time to their appearance before leaving for work.) and knows that he or she is being noticed and looked at strives hard to be noticeable in other ways too which gradually translates into confidence and a result oriented approach at work. Believe me, the "just out of bed" look does not impress colleagues. They would like to mix and work with someone who values themselves enough, to spend some time exclusively on themselves, be it on proper hygiene, preventing bad body odour and wearing clean and presentable clothes. For offices that have uniforms it becomes easier in terms of clothes selection but presentability is not limited to clothes alone, some time has to be allotted for this by you.

While browsing through the newspaper one day Sonia saw an advertisement and gave a call on that number. The tall girl who walked in from the front door 15 days later was indeed very presentable and well groomed. Yes, Sonia had taken an image consultant seriously and the PR Head in turn had taken her seriously. A new name that was added while making a list of event and social meet roles and responsibilities had Sonia as one of the Guest Relations Executives interacting with outsiders and employees. So could her capabilities and talent have undergone such a sea change in 15 days that her roles and responsibilities had also changed during Company social events? The answer would be a definite No. It was only the presentation that had changed not what lay within.

Your appearance is the preface of your story book, make it presentable and noticeable!

CHAPTER 26

THE LURE OF THE INANIMATE

I t would not be wrong to say that the workplace is rife with relationships both personal and professional within an organization; however we are more inclined towards and cherish the ones that are inanimate. The love of power, position, authority, moolah create a vortex of pull and become the epicenter for employee engagement. Bondings, goodwill, friendship are all sacrificed at the altar of career and monetary betterment. Appraisal times, new opportunities in your job, possibilities of a raise provide the perfect backdrop for such sightings.

Ram, Neha and Prabhu worked very closely as a team. Rarely had they given any other colleague room for gossip or complaint in either anything work related or personal. After the end of The Financial year in March, our company announced a new employee welfare and promotion activity through an overseas exchange programme. The selection process In India involved the submission of write ups by employees supported with relevant documents on the contribution that they had made in the past year, work wise, followed by a personal interview with the HR Head of the parent company in Greece. The enthusiasm and excitement was palpable in the office atmosphere as this meant a 1 year posting in the Head Quarters at Athens and a considerable hike in salary with a promotion on return to the India office. The religious fervor assumed an all time high with all employees in the running praying to their respective Gods and Goddesses to bless them with Athens. Team spirit, joint contributions, togetherness all flew out of the window as Ram Neha and Prabhu argued hard to present the work of the past year as their individual achievements. The corporate air was thick and heavy with me and mine, instead of his and ours. After the cases were presented, the three of them could not see eye to eye on anything trying to show how superior or more capable they were than the other person. This needless to stay stemmed from the powerful lure of what they saw as their individual gain in the company. "It can well be argued that for most of the working class it is either the moolah or power and authority that makes them tick so what was wrong here?"

In my opinion what emerged here was the brutal and merciless killing of the team spirit. You can still show your effectiveness by informing others about your contribution and not underplaying the other team mate's roles. Everybody would have contributed their bit for the final outcome. When the results came Ram, Neha and Prabhu featured nowhere on the list. In their haste to prove their efficiency they had negated the roles of their team mates and emphasized how individuals can be star performers and why credit should go to individuals and not teams, since discord in teams with unmatched capabilities of its members can be counterproductive and, how individuals can create better work results.

Ironically the position in Athens was titled "Senior Manager - Team development"

"Power and position are ephemeral and transient, what lasts a lifetime are your relationships. Sacrificing one for the other is like choosing death over life."

CHAPTER 27

INCLEMENT WEATHER AND A STRONG GUST OF SYCOPHANCY

The corporate globe has a mix of inhabitants who reside in different companies and practice different cultures. This particular breed that I bring to your attention is the Sycophants and hypocrites whose religion is to live by extolling the virtues of others albeit falsely. They are masters in this art and sharpen their skills with each passing day.

Swayam, the Finance Head of one of the Multinational companies I worked for was generally upbeat and carried an aura of great confidence with him in all that he did. With a successful career going, a sizeable team to lead and a career graph with a steep rise it was no wonder then that he gave in to a common human failing – that of providing a fertile ground for sowing the seeds of sycophancy. The worldly wise men and women in the company very soon understood on which side their bread was buttered. At business meetings, social gatherings he was raised on a pedestal by them and all that would reach his ears were words that extolled his leadership and professional skills. The biggest challenge of power they say is to use it wisely and Swayam displayed very poor control in this use. Biased decisions, preferential treatment of his favourites at work, misuse of company facilities and working hours became the done thing for him. The same Swayam who used to exude confidence at one time now exuded over confidence and misplaced authority. He became so unpopular that the only way to get through an easy and non controversial work life in that company was to humour him and play along with his whimsical ways at work. One fine day, the unthinkable happened – the external auditors discovered some anomalies in the book keeping and the misappropriation of official funds. The Top Management took this very seriously and Swayam was summoned to the Board room along with his team to explain and come clean.

When there is gross wrong doing and digital and physical footprints of the same there is very little to be said. Swayam could not and did not attempt to justify his actions. He knew his time was over and nothing that he would say would reverse his corporate misfortune.

I and all others present in the Board room that day understood the true meaning of short lived togetherness and the perils of sycophancy in its entirety. What unfolded inside was the complete detatchment of the same set of people who would hover around Swayam and pledge their undying loyalty in all that he said or did

Nobody stepped forward to even as much as open their mouth in a bid to defend his actions; they feigned complete ignorance of all the wrongs that they had been a party too along with him. What they probably saw in their minds' eye was the empty chair of the Finance Head and their own bright future. Nobody jumps onto a sinking ship and Swayam was indeed sinking. Sinking in the ocean of his own follies, submerged in the high tides of sycophancy which had made him lose sight of the corporate shore.

There is a fine line between praise and sycophancy, use your discretion to darken the line so that it remains clear and visible, letting your ego loose and unbridled will cloud and obliterate it !

CHAPTER 28

THE INTRICATE WEB OF MULTITASKING

The allure of Spiderman is not confined to just his super heroic exploits or the hours of fun and entertainment that his character provides, but resisting the charm of the spidey web and its powers can pose to be a big challenge for most of us. His inherent gift allows him to spin webs, swing to his advantage at opportune times, get out of tricky situations, and climb heights to overpower enemies. There is a Spiderman like quality in most of the corporate denizens. They are prone to believing that like this superhero they too have an inherent quality of multitasking and overpowering odds and deadlines. However, they are selective in wearing the spidey outfit and don it only for special occasions and only if instructions come from the top, for others like their subordinates or peers seeking their assistance the well rehearsed line of "I am very busy" is mouthed time and again till the person gives up and asks no more.

Ali was a sincere hard working boy and Smita was his female counterpart embodying similar skills. Both were popular with their seniors and had the endearing quality of never saying no to anyone. They had a smile for all corporate seasons and never seemed to tire of the tasks given to them, as a result of which they were the perfect dumping ground for all office chores and incomplete tasks of others.

Interestingly enough though, Ali who never said no to anyone and took on whatever was delegated or given to him was adept at using his discretion and attending to the tasks of only those that mattered, namely, anyone who was higher in rank and authority. Smita on the other hand remained untouched by this modus operandi and lapped up all the requests and instructions that came her way. As an approximation, at work they would be busy accommodating the requests of others for 7 hours out of the 9 at their disposal.

Reports, telephone calls, typing work, letters, ordering flowers for employee birthdays everything and anything came to them for execution. In fact we jokingly asked each other why they needed any specific designation or any specific department, a befitting designation could be Man Friday or Woman Friday reporting to the Multipurpose Department!

Over a cup of coffee I endeavored to peel off the outer layer of this multipurpose personality and ask Smita why she put her heart and soul into doing things for others which definitely did not occupy a space in her appointment letter. Pat came the reply - "It helps me to improve my knowledge and also sharpen my skills. I am so busy throughout the day that I don't waste time in gossiping or wasting time." Well, point noted, I moved on to Ali and posed the same question to him. He was honest enough to tell me that he did it to "please the bosses "and gain a career advantage. He said his logic was simple "If I don't say no to them how they can say no to me when I ask them for leave or a raise or an increment?" With this revelation of the ingredients for their perfect corporate recipe the thought that struck me was that it is not only the ingredients that contribute to the taste but the way in which they are blended and used.

I could see Ali trying his best to complete the tasks assigned to him scoring well in some, failing in a few, but what kept him going was his desire to create a perfect recipe. Smita on the other hand floundered on far too many occasions because she could not multitask a million tasks and her plate kept getting fuller and fuller till it spilled over and created a mess.

As for my style of working I do not draw inspiration from either Ali or Smita. I have realized that while one must be receptive to taking on additional jobs and responsibilities other than one's own at work, they should not focus on more than one task at a time because one cannot. Keep your plate full, but take one bite at a time was my self invented style of working.

Create and welcome a variety of food for your corporate appetite but opt for a three or four course meal with small sized bites. An unlimited buffet spread with an overfull plate may just end up choking you!

CHAPTER 29

THE ARTIST AND THE EASEL

The word romance has a myriad hues. Colour and fluidity are its hallmarks. If I were to draw a parallel I would say that throughout your career you are the artist constantly playing with colours that your vision shapes. As you step onto the corporate canvas, your footprints leave a distinct impression. My initial days of self discovery and discovery of my career partner had multiple hues of bright colours to more sober ones to really dull and drab ones. We even discovered some in between colours Gred (Grey + Red) being one. This particular one was characterized with dull boring grey moments interspersed with bright and happy ones. One particular outstation programme to a nearby destination created an ample opportunity for us to exploit our interests and learn more about each other. I could spend hours trying to match my professional capabilities with the profession itself, for instance there was a press meet I had to organize and create the required paraphernalia for it. I just had to stretch out my hand to my career partner and embark on this voyage of discovery holding an eternal promise of togetherness. Thus began the conceptualization of the event, issuing of invites, setting the stage for the interactions, planning the press kits and drafting press releases, briefing the team and the Top Management who would be taking on the questions. Experiencing an adrenaline rush and breathing a million breaths in one minute we painted our canvas with all the colours of brightness. Enthusiam, anticipation and togetherness create a wonderful assortment of brightness. My career partner and I were blinded by our love for what we were doing. We had eyes for nobody or nothing else. It was our professional togetherness at an all time high. This feeling lasted for a couple of years and on a couple of occasions, we also faced certain days when things were not very good despite our perfect planning and those were the grey and brown days of my career. A particular instance comes to my mind when I had left for a meeting not too far away from my office but the meeting itself turned out to be a damp squib making me question the need for even attempting to drive all the distance. What transpired within the cabin of the other office was nothing spectacular in fact it could well have been discussed over phone and I left with no take aways or food for thought to nibble on. Then there were those days when colleagues got into big arguments and a volley of words were the only thing you could recollect as you settled down to bed. Those black and dark days were certainly days you wished could be wiped out of your corporate memory.

Each occasion, each relationship adds a new colour to your canvas, remember it's your hand that is holding the brush that can create strokes of visual delight and appeal both for the artist and the viewer.

CHAPTER 30

FLIGHT TO CENTRE STAGE MANY CLIPPED WINGS LATER

Most success stories that I have heard have the proverbial "Rags to riches" storyline, so when my corporate career was following a steady annual increment growth a feeling of restlessness started seeping in. "Would this be my future? Would my small joys be limited between the 10 – 20 % salary raise or would something more exciting happen?" A new determination like never before starting setting in as I realized that I was meant for much more. Having introduced you to my mental role plays and fertile imagination earlier, it would not surprise you if I told you that I took recourse to that once again. I worked out a mental pattern where I would don several caps other than my own and put myself in different shoes and enact different roles and parts.

There was an annual budget meeting which used to take place in my first company which apart from the numbers to be looked at and discussed had the lure of exotic destinations that the team members would take off to for the purpose of these deliberations and to arrive at a common consensus. The byes and take cares echoed in my ears as the travelling team members bade goodbye to us the lonely crusaders in office. Not feeling very good about being left out of this I wondered why everybody well not if everybody at least a sizeable majority in the office could not contribute towards these budgetary decisions. Weren't all of us in our own ways utilizing the office allocated budgets? Electricity, office hours, conveyance, provisions and so on. In my opinion at least 2 members from each department not necessarily based on seniority should have been included for their view points; however, this very individual view point of some seniors ensured that my suggestion was vetoed out when I had suggested it earlier. An uncanny peculiar characteristic of mine has been to try and achieve things which I have great conviction about and which are denied to me, I am happy to say that 90 % of the times this has worked in my favour though. This particular incident too made me contemplate on my next course of action to take me closer to my goal. The next couple of months were devoted to being a part of all the discussions that took place with even a remote connection to cost saving measures in the office and I started helping my seniors with their presentations and talks and needless to say it was well accepted as they felt I had a flair for it and could make their lives easier. So well ingrained did this PR angle of my job become with this particular corporate way of life that for the next time's budget meeting, the location, hotels, tickets, Presentations everything found a new route – my desk!

The team that left next year then bade farewell and mouthed take cares to fewer people since a majority of us were headed to Singapore!

A foregone conclusion of any job is that anybody who is employed reports to someone unless you are the owner of the company. This reporting structure can either be a stumbling block for you or add a fillip to your career depending on whom and how your boss is. The corporate crowd is sectioned into employees who are the blue eyed boys or girls and enjoy a wonderful rapport with and encouragement from the boss. Then there is the section that is always at loggerheads with their superiors with frayed tempers and unproductivity on the rise. Then there are those who are focused only on their 9 to 5 role and seldom venture into anything contentious and just clock in and clock out.

My career started the usual way then developed a steep incline with me assuming additional roles and responsibilities. Gradually I became quite central to all corporate activities. Time for a change of department and a new boss. Roger was everything that a boss should not be. Insecure, unpunctual, slow on the uptake, laid back and generally unpleasant. A female employee in his opinion had to be dealt with caution since we according to him could dangle the sexual harassment bait to suit our purposes. He would never see any female employee alone in his cabin we had to necessarily walk in with a colleague whether or not he or she was involved in the discussion. In the absence of colleagues, the office boy would be there serving the eternal unending cups of tea. I sometimes wondered whether the protective layer of security was because he was unsure of all that was feminine or all that was himself? That could not be discovered till date since none of us actually got down to asking him.

There was an exhibition scheduled for Taiwan and we as a department put in a lot of effort and time in preparing for it. The final participation list was drawn out and circulated. There were 5 women in the department and 4 males. The list included only the males. All the women felt terrible at being sidelined and approached Roger with the obvious question of why not them? His only reaction was a simple "No" the names and he rattled of all the male ones "are better presenters and can handle the visitors better." I was looking forward to this opportunity but felt dejected and could almost sense how a caged bird with wings clipped would feel. This was one such occasion but there were so many others where the X and Y were pitted against each other pronounced and distinct never to merge.

Well I thought it was time to change the course of things and I decided to write out a letter to Roger's superior. A few days later I was invited into the cabin of the superior and I attempted to explain the entire functioning and the high dejection levels prevalent within the department. The next day I along with a few other women were reporting to another boss who thankfully embodied all that was Rogers' opposite. I was given a free hand to implement my ideas (of course after sounding it out to the team and my boss) and things started looking up. With my creative genius in place and many opportunities that I didn't let slip by I started being noticed as a performer and a woman of substance who worked hard and was also a good team player.

A year later the team was slated to visit and participate in another exhibition in Spain, the list was drawn up and this time there were 5 male members and 4 females including me. Roger chose not to participate feigning as we came to know later, a last minute urgent family engagement.

Spread out your wings with the grit and determination needed for flying taking extreme care not to succumb to the passiveness of getting them clipped!

CHAPTER 31

KNOW YOUR NO

Most of us would agree with the fact that the word No symbolizes everything that is negative and does not hold you in good stead in front of others. Viewed differently, one can safely agree though that there is a wonder and positivity attached to the word No. Let us attempt a deliberation on the word in all its dimensions, and what better way than running through a few situations.

Ira was a very popular girl who with her good looks and attractive personality had created a circle of admirers within the corporate fraternity, males and females included. She was an endearing girl ready to help people and always on the go and very accommodative as far as work was concerned. When such people go out on company tours they necessarily get the best of everything. The hotels and guest relations staff go out of their way to offer freebies to them, the colleagues who travel with them also look forward to such trips with work and pleasantness combined.

Ira had to take a trip to Delhi and the male and female colleagues at the Delhi office were elated to hear of her visit. Delhi having acquired the unsafe title in capital letters for female travelers especially at night saw her male colleagues calling her up asking her whether she wanted to be picked up from the airport. Not wanting to say no to either of them and in the process hurting them she agreed to their offer. As a result of which there were 3 cars with 3 drivers to pick up one girl. It was obvious that they hadn't exchanged notes with each other nor had she deemed it fit to inform any of them about the other callers. Many embarrassed and surprised looks later Delhi airport witnessed a beautiful lady being escorted by 3 men getting into one car, the overnight parking fee for 3 cars was inconsequential in comparison to the one and a half hours drive to the hotel in the company of a radiant and smiling Ira. Whew, what a waste of resources and time even Ira would reluctantly admit if only the no had been said in time!

Then there are the corporate citizens who take great pride in the fact that they have never said no to any work in life. As a result of which they appear perpetually overloaded. They are the ones who stretch the office hours beyond the scheduled ones and gradually progress into the next day sitting on their desks with piles and piles of tasks to attend to. They are the or as they would like to believe the "hard working lot "as opposed to the hardly working ones. Mr. Kurien had self bracketed himself into the first lot.

Mrs Kurien and the baby Kuriens had a lot against the company which seemed to swallow their husband and father for long hours. Kurien took solace in the fact that he was supporting his family and giving them all that was needed for a comfortable living based on the hours of his hard work so that the company would value him and the chances of his job security were polished and brightened.

Getting underneath the surface of this what was discovered and understood by the smart ones was that although Kurien was a bright hard working guy he had actually started taking on and completing the tasks assigned to others so that he could stay in everybody's good books. He took immense pride in the fact that he was hailed as a helpful and extremely cooperative colleague. Well, who would not call you cooperative if you had a movie to watch and only your work could have prevented you and you suddenly discovered this accommodative ever smiling Kurien to take on your tasks with the promise of completion before you came back the next day.

By making way for others family lives and personal engagements to progress unhindered after office hours Kurien had unknowingly given birth to the shoulder syndrome where people would lean on him for support. The shoulder itself with so much work load started sagging till it eventually drooped and dislocated itself from its own family and "me time." Mrs. Kurien and baby Kuriens decided to call it a day as they moved back to their home town and their native village saying, they preferred being surrounded by the company of their friends and relatives, if it was only the pay check that came to them from Kurien it could as well travel all the way to the native village.

Not everything about No is negative, positive outcomes emerge when you know when to use it!

CHAPTER 32

THE DISPENSABLE INDISPENSABLE

A peculiar mid career occurrence is a feeling of contentment coupled with the pronounced "feet firmly" planted label. Mr. Rao had served a good 15 years in his company and was well entrenched in the system, wading through various corporate nuances with ease and fluidity. He was the person to approach during any crisis, any approvals, any suggestions and any decisions, having served so many loyal and fruitful years within the company.

Words like punctuality, attendance, deadlines gradually started diminishing in importance for him. It was a common feature to see his chair vacant till noon before he occupied it and then within an hour breezed out. He would put in hours at work and complete his tasks but not as per the company timings and protocol but as per his convenience. This was perceived by employees in different ways. Those reporting to him and working in close association with him acquired the privilege club membership by default, exempt from adherence to office timings, not governed by the number of leaves and other general guidelines labeled as official. The other lot was the disgruntled, unhappy with a "why do some people have all the privileges? kind of look.

It is said that one must not stretch ones' luck too far and never could it have been truer as in this case of Mr Rao and his little fiefdom.

This particular company was an owner driven one and a family owned business with the underlying unwritten rule of one king one kingdom.

One day, the vacant chair of Mr. Rao continued to stare us in the eye without any trace of its occupant. The privilege club members who trickled in slowly throughout the day started getting restless with no signs of their king and no contact with him.

Ram the office boy ran in two days later with the news that Mr. Rao had decided to take voluntary retirement. We wondered as to how he knew this and he informed us that he had heard our HR Head speaking with the Chairman while Ram was cleaning his cabin. Shell shocked at this news the various sections of the staff, the privilege club, the downtrodden low morale ones, the turning a blind eye blinkered ones, all shook their heads and sighed for various reasons. Some with relief, some with this is the way of the world, and some in despair at the absence of their Godfather, but all of them knew and admitted openly or discreetly that designations and people all had a corporate shelf life, some with the natural process of retirement, some with the premature imposed one called voluntary retirement.

Words can be re written and letters re arranged. The prefix "in" in indispensable is itself dispensable.

CHAPTER 33

OF DEMI GODS AND EGO BOOSTERS

God is the creator of this universe and the corporate universe is the creator of Demi Gods. The corporate universe with all its offerings of power and perks provides the perfect breeding ground for power struck egoistic individuals.

Naina joined the reputed Multinational Company as a front office executive; this hardworking sincere girl was noticed and rewarded for her sincerity and dedication to work with a promotion in the marketing department. New responsibilities, a new team to lead and unlimited interactions with the Managing Director and other Senior Management saw Naina move on to the higher rungs of the coporate ladder not only in terms of designation but also communication. The Top Management welcomes the idea of a responsible intermediary conveying things to the employees. Naina was the chosen one here and nobody had so much access to the Chairman and MD as Naina. She would walk in and out of their offices and their homes with a sense of purpose and the determination to make the others sense her importance in the organization.

People were wary of her, all gossip and all negative thoughts and ideas were kept at bay and in wraps from her since everybody knew that it would not take long for it to travel to the ears of the bosses and nobody wanted to risk their jobs or their wrath.

It was Naina, Naina all the way. Requests and suggestions all followed the implicit rule of sounding out Naina and then requesting her to follow it through. Nina was Naina's junior and was hardworking and dedicated to her job. A few kilometres away from the office was a convent school which Naina's 4 year old daughter attended. One Friday afternoon while in office Nina received a call from Naina informing her that she was still 2 hours away from the office and it was the pickup time of her daughter from school and since Shaina her daughter had met Nina before and knew her she would readily agree to accompany her, so could she just hop across and pick up Shaina. Much to everybody's surprise and I am sure a big shock to Naina, Nina refused this saying it was during office hours and she could not run personal errands. This of course did not go down well with Naina but she let it pass at that time.

This company had a rule that annual leave for LTA (Leave Travel Allowance) should have the concurrence of your immediate superior along with the approval of the Chairman. I personally think this was done as a strict measure to ensure that employees did not misuse this facility since it was encashable and the thought of it reaching the top most person would act as a deterrent for any malpractice since it would be subject to scrutiny if anything foul was sensed.

Naina got her usual set of requests and applications which she in turn took to the Chairman. On her exit from the cabin she handed out the approvals and one rejection, - Nina's. Nina immediately sought an audience with the Chairman with the intention of finding out the reason since it was well in keeping with the company policy. The Chairman asked her to step in with Naina. The aura of the Chairman was enough to make her tongue tied and nothing emerged beyond the "I want to talk to you Sir...." the impatient and busy

Chairman immediately shot a rejoinder of "speak to Naina about it." After coming out of the cabin Naina shot a steely look in her direction and said – "You can't go next door during office hours can you? So how can we allow you to absent yourself from work for 15 days? The Accounts dept will calculate your entitlement and add it in your pay packet for next month but unfortunately you will not be permitted to undertake any real time travel, therefore no leave or absenteeism from work will be permitted. I truly feel sorry for you but can't be helped." Nina's self esteem told her not to react and give Naina more reason to gloat by fanning her sense of vindication. You can only reason with the reasonable and request the sensible and Naina was neither.

Another flip side is that when men or women perform well in their jobs they get intangible and tangible benefits. While praise, compliments and goodwill are welcome they can either fan the ego and have a negative influence on you or instill a sense of self confidence to propel you to perform better.

Comparison is something that is generally negative when you compare yourself with others as a bargaining edge for any salary hikes or increments, rather than using it as a benchmark and tool to measure your success to work harder and perform better.

The ones who are at the receiving end of the company perks, tangible and intangible benefits, have a difficult time exercising restraint and not allowing it to go to their heads. A few succeed a few don't, with the scale dipping more towards the latter.

Saket as The MD of a leading Manufacturing company had the best of things that corporate life could offer. The super luxury cars in which he and his family moved with élan, the retinue of servants and security guards at home were all company provided.

The visits to the grocery store, provisions shopping, dropping the children to school were all done by the different cars and drivers at his disposal. His pet dog too had a car assigned for his visit to the vet or walks in the parks.

This perk culture grew very comfortably as a second skin on him and his family members.

The Company's performance started dipping in the volatile market and sustaining a top heavy organization became a challenge. In less than a month Saket was eased out of the organization. Without the paraphernalia of cooks, guards and fancy cars life for him and his family became miserable.

Ego trips and demigod status are short lived and ephemeral what lasts is your self worth and godly deeds!

CHAPTER 34

SOCIAL TRESPASSES – GUFFAWS AND GOOF UPS!

M ost of us if not all from the working class would like to believe that we are in tune with the changing times. With the modern world unleashing technology and almost slamming it hard on our faces, keeping abreast of it is an outdated concept, staying ahead is the need of the hour. "Shape up or ship out" would never ring more true than it does in modern times.

Ram the new joinee, was adept at using gadgets and gizmos and led a technologically advanced life whereas Shyam his boss and much senior in years was still finding his bearings through the maze and criss crossed paths of whats app, instagram, twitter, linked in and facebook. Human beings rarely make public admissions of their intellectual poverty and the same was the case here. Shyam would look in amazement at the alacrity and speed at which the fingers of Ram would move on the cell phone or laptop. Knowledge of technology and his deftness with gizmos gave Ram the professional advantage which he lacked in terms of age and experience. Shyam at a 50 + stage of life was still very active and keen to match up to the modern technological advancements so a few informal lessons later he was part of the department whats app group. He felt a new thrill envelope him with the everyday exchanges of official reminders, information on meetings, an occasional joke or two, birthday wishes and so on.

Raj was a promising young employee and one of Shyam's favourites, a perfect employee for being showcased as a living example of dedication, sincerity, hard work and all things good. He had been recently selected for the employee exchange programme in Barcelona and also been given a company cell phone and laptop to make communication easier while he was on his two month trip away from India. The day of his departure dawned and he was to come for a while to the office before leaving for the airport. We set about our routine tasks and Shyam soon realized that Raj had not come in as yet. We were told to check on his whereabouts but we could not come up with an answer because we could not establish contact with him. About half an hour later we saw a fuming and fretting Shyam walk up to us and announce loudly that he never expected Raj to behave this way. He had to as per the company protocol come and collect his papers and files before he left. Treading very cautiously on this fuming verbal territory I managed to ask in a soft voice how he had come to know. Shyam just kept waving his hands in the air and pointing to his phone. Presuming that Raj had sent him a personal message announcing his departure we too were a little taken aback since the office was enroute the airport and he could have stopped by to bid his goodbyes. Anyway, work had to carry on and we went back to our respective desks, no sooner had we settled in that we saw the object of our contemplation and discussion walking in with a smile. Our mouths wide open we looked at him incredulously hadn't he left was the unspoken question on our lips and more so on Shyam's lips. "Have you all seen a ghost guys what's up with you all?" asked Raj. "Well hadn't you messaged Shyam that you had left?" I asked him "No certainly not" he said. "I was very much in office changing my sim card to my new hand set, configuring my groups and contacts" "but then, what about this?" shouted out Shyam very loudly pointing to his phone. We all crowded around and focused on what was written on his screen "Raj left" Trying to stifle our laughter we looked at each other and understood that this exit was indeed from the group and not the country!

The lighting speed of communication with technology also causes a lot of embarrassment like instances when wrong forwards and wrong messages reach the unintended recipient. Faux paxes and bloopers leave you red faced as you are hit with this bolt of realization on many an occasion.

Resignations, appointments, break ups, make ups, are all so conveniently packed in this mode of social media communication.

On the brighter side you don't have to pick up the phone to actually convey humor or bonding texts and emoticons serve the purpose well.

Use social media wisely – the choice of being labeled social or anti social lies in your fingertips!

CHAPTER 35

CORPORATE ZOMBIES

S trange are the ways of the world and some peoples' claim to fame. You see them walk past lost in their own world and any question you pose to them will be met with blank expressions so preoccupied are they with their own thoughts. These are the employees who are so hard working (or so they say) that they don't have time to breathe, leave alone sleep.

The list of virtues and vices that have been our legacy from time immemorial has undergone numerous additions and deletions over the years, but one constant which is highlighted time and again is the always alert tribe, advocating and supporting insomnia.

I am by nature the edgy types to clarify further, edgy for work and its responses. If I am given a task I ensure that it gets the required appropriate response and I am at tenterhooks till it is done. Sleep must follow its usual pattern but I do believe that one must sleep only to refresh and rejuvenate oneself and not sleep to while away time. I have therefore never been tempted to join the eternally awake work exploited fraternity. You will encounter them everywhere, walking with dazed expressions, not responding to your questions till they are shaken out of their stupor. Encounters of the close kind will reveal that they have so much work that they do not know how to cope with it except by staying awake and working. Now the million dollar question which, pops up is it work that they are doing or trying to battle sleep that overcomes them whilst losing out on productive work time?

Lara was the always ready for tasks types and could be seen hustling and bustling around the office spaces with a million things to do. Nothing in the office escaped her attention, a tubelight that wasn't working to an un ironed uniform to the regular work chores in all its intricacies. She was as perfect as can be in trying to execute her regular tasks and even those beyond her call of duty.

She took great pride in bagging the best employee, best attendance and so many other awards which paid obeisance to her never say die attitude and called for her perpetual attentiveness at work.

In fact she was a 24 x7 attendant for all that was needed. When an employees' car broke down well past midnight and she was stranded on the highway, the number on speed dial was Lara's and as expected, she was quickly bailed out of this trying situation. People would not hesitate to call her at any time on any day of the week or year for she would be the one point contact for all work. Terms and words like afternoon siestas, power naps, holiday switch offs were unheard of for her as she was always accessible and perpetually awake both physically and mentally for all requests and work coming her way.

Although a strong advocator of the always alert category I propagate a few reservations there. I would intersperse this line with a shut eye to read as - being alert, having a shut eye, and alert again. Lara was to take off to Hong Kong for a business meeting and her flight was scheduled to depart at 0030 hrs. Being a workaholic as she was, she continued working throughout the day and throughout the evening, on the day of her travel. On arriving at the airport she took a seat far away from her boarding gate since the boarding gate hadn't opened as yet and most of the seats were already occupied. Immersed in her work on her laptop and a few calls later, she slipped into sweet slumber a natural phenomenon which she had been denying herself for far too long. While she soothed her frayed nerves and tired body with this blissful sleep, there were others who walked past her to immigration and beyond….. The boarding gate opened, remained open for a good 3- 4 hours and closed again with the final boarding announced. Her sleep deprived body made the most of the gift bestowed on it and she continued sleeping oblivious to the passage of time. You gain some, you lose some, they say but here this loss could well have been avoided. People like Lara who probably think that being tired is a badge of honor, should realize that it actually saps you of your mental alertness and productivity. Apparently although you are awake and working, your mental doors and receptiveness have already shut out the work that you are doing. Lara had been so busy and alert to others' needs and requirements that she had skipped paying attention to her own and had lost out on something very important and crucial by missing her flight.

If somebody tells you about their long working hours and how they have taxed their eyelids by not allowing them to close, spare a moment to tell yourself how with all their talk of effectiveness and self swagger they have ended up being unproductive and dim. Not only have they harmed their own productivity but may have also unleashed negativity on all who came in their contact by way of their rudeness, lack of patience and so on because these are the ornaments of the sleep deprived employees. By embracing the normal natural pattern of sleep you will not compromise on your health and creativity and most importantly be a better employee and a better boss.

Give each stage and each activity of nature its due importance. What would you like to accessorize your work personality with? Designer bags of productivity and goodwill or self branded bags under your eyes?

CHAPTER 36

A SARTORIAL DREAM

A look at his crisp shirt and well ironed pants with designer shoes and belts to match would have set many a hearts aflutter. A collection of designer brands as accompaniments of his arrival in office were a common phenomenon, in fact as acceptable as the rising and setting of the sun. The man who had walked into a small office 25 years ago was in no way comparable to this man driving around in his flashy convertible with a chauffeur in attendance. That man Someshwar was in stark contrast to this one, as he clutched on to his dreams and determination and the little suitcase that he had bought from his mothers savings. He sat in a nondescript seat of the 3 tier compartment of the train making his way to Mumbai the city which had the reputation of playing God Mother to every Cinderella and their male counterparts.

Someshwar hardly got the opportunity to open his file full of paper qualifications including a topper's certificate from his Engineering College; he would never reach to that stage because just a glance at him would make the HR Managers come up with various reasons to dismiss him from the pre interview room itself. It was the age of the Multinationals and the opening of global doors in India. Where "Namastes" gave way to hi and heys, when some women took certain cost saving measures so seriously at work that they replaced their long six yards of sari with short skirts, where men started sporting French beards and hiring tailors who were well informed about the latest office wear styles, all this in a bid to keep pace with the changing global environment and raise their employability quotient.

Someshwar with his traditional pair of slippers, oiled hair and nerdy look was considered unemployable even before he could open his mouth. These Multinationals had a reputation to keep, how could an employee looking like he did meet their overseas counterparts. In a bid to justify their patriotism lest fingers be pointed, the HR Managers would say they were patriotic and Indian but "fish out of water?" nay, how could they employ such people where the initial gap was so evident that it would curtail further interaction. Wouldn't it be detrimental for the company?

Having encountered so many no's in his job endeavours he had almost resigned himself to the fate of a city returned guy and was about to board the evening train back to his native village when he decided to give one last shot to the Executive Finance's advertised vacancy with walk in interviews that day at a leading Manufacturing company where I happened to be a part of the interview team.

As the Receptionist announced the lineup of candidates I couldn't but help notice the sudden drop in her tone while introducing him, it was almost as if she were saying "come on try your luck but we know what you are in for." It was probably this introduction itself which made me look up and notice the entry of Someshwar. I could see a twinkle in his eye and a sincere smile beneath his dejected exterior, on prompting him to introduce himself he did it surprisingly with great élan and aplomb. The majority of us in the interview committee were of the opinion that he should be given a chance while all others had their different reasons mine was driven with the compelling desire to initiate him into the exciting world of Image Management.

Veracity finds a footing in the saying that reel life takes off from real life, and I could in my mind's eye see the scene of the famous movie Pretty Woman unfold, the scene where Julia Roberts as Vivian is refused waiting upon at the Beverly Hills store – Boulmiche, just because she doesn't look as a potential client of theirs should look. Someshwar was denied an audience at meetings and an ear at social gatherings just because he didn't look like one of us. We would like to believe that we shun pretension and don't go by first appearances but even as we say that we know that it rings rather untrue more so in the corporate world.

Working on diction, accent, clothing, body language and posture was an enriching experience for both of us and we were more than happy at our handiwork and the outcome as the shunned and rejected Someshwar transformed into the well accepted Sam.

This was the birth, conception, addition and integration of another rewarding link into my PR career – Image Management.

Adopt the Outside In approach. You can show people the talent and creativity that you house inside only if you appeal to them from the outside.

CHAPTER 37

THE CORPORATE HIDE

While your corporate journey brings out different facets of your personality, it also endows you with an enviable exterior. This process of metamorphosis is an integral part of your corporate life. When you join you are at your vulnerable best and prone to emotional and mental attacks, till you gradually learn that not everyone will like you, no matter what you do, so it is best to mix with people who will appreciate your presence rather than wasting time on people who don't.

My eyes shone with excitement and my heart raced faster than usual as I stretched out my hand to greet the new Chairman from our parent company in Athens. He had decided to spend two months at the India office and look into the day to day affairs. There was nothing very Chairmanly and distant about him I thought to myself as I instantly took a liking to his corporate personality and I could see that the feeling was mutual. Our tuning at work was perfect and I enjoyed working for him as much as he enjoyed handing out work to me.

The human mind is complex and the phrase "pure" enjoyment is yet something that is just mouthed and not really taken much note of in the etymological way. I have learnt as a result of constant exposure that purity per say will be adulterated in peoples' mind. Soon, there were conjectures on our close association and every corporate advancement of mine was attributed to ***that*** certain closeness. During the initial years I would take on the cudgel of admonishing these by step by step explanations, but soon realized that I wasn't making much headway there.

Then, something magical happened. I could feel a growing sense of detachment pervade my exterior, it was as if your head was exposed to water with a shower cap ensuring that your hair remained dry. The few drops of water that would manage a sly entry were easily shaken off and did not affect your hair style.

I imbibed many valuable lessons during this short interaction, the most valuable being the **corporate hide**. This protective cover ensures that all the grime and dust of conjectures, rumors, jibes, barbed comments are kept at bay and do not permeate the sensitive skin below.

Kamat was a senior manager who was a self proclaimed favourite of the Chairman and a cause of envy by others. He also drew the comments and ire of other employees but on a different account than mine, with the gender issue raising its small ugly head here. A man can be close close but a woman can't be close close, you see.

It was a Thursday meeting where Kamat, The Chairman and I were present. Midway through the meeting the Chairman realized that the work had not progressed as per his instruction and there were many avoidable gaps. It was a first of its kinds when I saw him lose his cool and admonish Kamat well and proper in a loud booming voice. The meeting ended sooner than expected as Kamat was told to leave the cabin and come back only after he had completed the work according to what had been agreed.

It was time for me to leave for the day and I was winding up my routine work. One of my end of the day tasks was replaying the recording from the security cameras placed at various strategic locations in the office and save it in a folder kept exclusively for that purpose to be played back as and when needed.

What I witnessed in the recording of Kamat walking out of the Chairman's office and to the pantry and his cabin thereafter filled me with an initial shock, fading into a sense of wonder and amazement. Outside the Chairman's door I saw a physical gesture of Kamat symbolically dusting his jacket as if something had fallen on it, dusting all the negativity of harsh words and then walking past with a smile. He was greeting all those who came in his way and smiling at his juniors as he walked into the pantry made his cup of tea and walked back to his cabin and settled down to work. The smile and pleasantness never left his face till he disappeared from the eye of the camera.

Kamat had indeed practiced to hide (pun intended) unpleasantness by not making public through his actions and reactions of what had transpired inside the cabin, to his ever curious colleagues and his physical gesture of brushing off the words of the Chairman outside the door had actually given him the confidence to carry on with his work without taking the negativity with him.

Though every employee is in the public domain of the company, our career also gives us a safe deposit vault to store our valuable assets which are not visible to the others. The corporate hide is a welcome asset for those who can opt for it and can be made operational during our working hours, to be locked and stored safely within the personal deposit locker of our corporate personality after work.

CHAPTER 38

THE DEMON OF GUILT PANGS

D o you label guilt as an emotion, or an obstacle, a hindrance to your purpose or something which you can absorb and move ahead without, is it something which you can remain absolutely unfazed and untouched by? During my career, I have attempted several definitions and can now safely in my opinion attempt a final, much worked on, time tested one.

Your career all said and done sometimes makes you feel apologetic for something that you did or thought about at some point of time or the other, how you manage those is the skill which marks your personality.

During the initial days when I walked into a profession which had various connotations and interpretations of the word "Public" associated with it the arduous task of working on various presumptions also unfolded before me. The look Mr. Mehta gave as I stepped into his cabin during my first job, would have made even the strongest and bravest of souls cringe. My entry into the all male dominated bastion of the corporate department unleashed myriad expressions which I did not even attempt to count. I experienced my first corporate guilt pang at that time, on my decision. Time flew and he gradually started looking past the initial divide of my physical form and womanly attributes to the stronger foundations of my work results and I gradually gained acceptance.

Jamina looked as much a boy as all her male colleagues with her sense of dressing, her hairstyle and the way she carried herself complete with their mannerisms and her voice too which proved to be a strong alibi making it very difficult to differentiate her from them till you actually saw her in person. That was her way of being gender effective and admonishing her guilt pangs.

Then there are the usual tch tchs haws and hums to contend with when a working woman embraces motherhood, contemplations that range from necessity and desperation to work due to financial compulsions to downright condemnation at the callousness towards the health and well being of the unborn child.

Ragini still single but contemplating marriage, was quite infuriated at the judgments and dismissals by others that made up any expectant working mothers universe, and she had in her own way tried to reason out with whoever she knew that they had a life beyond being a full time inactive expectant mother. That particular day when there was huge queue at the first day first show of a popular concert, Ragini knew she stood no chance of an entry before the gate closed. The thought that crossed her mind was if she should beat people at their own game? All it needed was a few rummages in her duffle bag and she was ready for her part. Ragini sped past the long queue with great ease and alacrity, all it needed to work was the magical duo of a baby bump (created by the scarves and sweater present in her duffle bag) and peoples sympathies. This guilt pang as she reasoned out to herself was created by the people, for a pregnant woman had to necessarily feel guilty if she was doing something beyond the expected realms of society – and what happened here was no sympathy it was more of a "let's not be a party to the sinner by allowing her to collapse while queuing up for long."

Our career too unleashes many instances when we take decisions, support people and exercise our judgment on various occasions. Guilt pangs come as accompaniments, sometimes. We must attempt to own the results of any actions that we take as much as we own our successes, and guilt pangs must never make an inroad on the roadmap of our actions.

The demon of guilt feeds on our vulnerability, but when your mind and body close the doors and cordon it off, it remains hungry and deprived!

CHAPTER 39

NUDGES AND EDGES

T here is an interesting parallel to be drawn between the thrill of adventure sports and a rewarding career. The early years see all of us armed with a zillion ways of action but lacking the boldness of execution.

Rajeshwari my colleague was as much a part of the departmental Monday meetings as me that we would have with our counterparts in Boston with our Clocks and watched adjusted to accommodate a convenient different time zone telephone call. There would be notes in front of all the participants and the agenda for discussion typed and discussed well in advance. On the third such instance, she hesitantly mentioned to me that the pattern of this call could be changed. With all of us trying to make ourselves audible to faceless people we could actually connect on a skype or a video conference call and see each other, gauge each other's reactions and limit and curtail the high decibel levels which inevitably became a recurring midway phenomenon (after a few initial exchanges were done) in a bid to be heard over each other. I am taking you back to a good many years when Skype and video conferencing had just about emerged and were yet unheard of in the corporate corridors. Rajeshwari herself had come in from the US and was well versed with this. The question that loomed large here was who would bell the cat? We were both new and eager to make a mark in the "taking initiative and smart category," but unwilling to be a part of the "tried and failed category." The third meeting progressed to the fourth without any changes or suggestions. On the fifth occasion after a heavy downpour the telephone lines went dead that is the regular telephone line and not the one on which our wi fi operated. A few solemn faces and sighs later, when everybody started wondering how to carry on the Monday review meeting, Rajeshwari gathered the courage to voice her thoughts on a Skype or video call.

A few who were unwilling to deviate from the tried and tested route rejected this immediately however there were a few who were keen to experiment, this set of people proceeded to the conference room. Minutes later, with everything in place a Skype account was created, our Boston team informed and the meeting was initiated. The entire process was seamless and stood much higher in terms of the quality of interaction. Kudos and accolades were in order for Rajeshwari by the entire team. All it needed was a push by technology to adopt an improved and more effective version of it!

Kapil our junior accountant came from a small village in Kerala and every morning he walked into his office with the same reverence that he would into a place of worship. He was the only earning member in a family of 7, with his mother and paralytic father and 5 dependant sisters. This job was the only source of livelihood for him and his family but he referred to it as God's blessing in abundant measure for a simple God fearing man. There was great excitement at work since we had our first soon to be inaugurated International branch in Dubai. Work moved at a hectic pace for all departments as each was given an assignment to be completed and directed to the team there. The Accounts department was a crucial one in the scheme of things and as bad luck would have it, the HOD Finance met with an accident while coming to office and was declared unfit to attend office for a month. Kapil was asked to take charge and execute all pending work. Many late nights, and a lot of hard work later Kapil presented the assignment on behalf of his department.

The next day Kapil was summoned to the Managing Directors' cabin. It took him a long time to muster enough courage to walk inside the imposing doors. He was always the "behind the scene" boy and had never ever spoken to the Top Management, leave alone the MD in his one year of employment. He was so nervous that he fumbled with his wishes and could barely speak a word in front of the Managing Director. So numb was he with apprehension that the words of the Head HR "you have done exceedingly well and we are pleased to inform you that we are offering you a promotion as Senior Accountant with a transfer to our Dubai office, and would like to discuss it further with you." failed to evoke any reaction except a deadpan expression. After a couple of "Kapil are you okay?" sentences, was he shaken out of his stupor to respond with a feeble yes. He was still in a state of shock as he walked out expressionless and dazed.

A hurried phone call home to apprise his family of the developments and a torrent of congratulatory remarks from colleagues at work made him finally realize what had happened. It took him a long time to understand that if he accepted the offer he would have to leave his one year old workplace and his current work life with all its associations and his native home which was just a train ride away. After much deliberation, he decided to reject the offer. He was gradually making his way to the Head HRs cabin to announce that his current comfort zone had outweighed the lure of Dubai when his cell phone rang seeing "Home calling" on his screen in bold letters he stepped back to answer the call. It was his father at the other end. Mr Naidu hardly spoke so dejected was he with his ailing condition, that words were a rarity. This call that he made to his son was a crucial one. He reasoned out with Kapil on how good the offer was and how he could trace a great career path which apart from enriching him in very possible way would also be a boon for the family. Mr Naidu must have imparted some wonderful advice to Kapil, as his face lit up after he disconnected the call. His steps became surer and firmer, faster and more confident as he covered the short distance to the Head HR's cabin. His knock on the door sounded a confident YES for Dubai. Kapil was just at the edge of a decision, his father proved to be a catalyst in hastening it and taking it to a positive and successful closure.

Our career topography is dotted with ravines, deep gorges, plateaus and cliffs. While tracing our path we may encounter hostile or unfamiliar territory. We have to push ourselves to cross that and move ahead either by the power of our inner resources or by the power of somebody else's nudge. Being at the edge is another challenging aspect.

The difference between success and failure is defined by a single step. One wrong step and you fall at breakneck speed to a bottomless pit while the right one gives you the wings to soar and fly!

CHAPTER 40

NARCISSISM REDEFINED

All corporate citizens are aware and familiar with people who display a grandiose sense of self, violate social norms, break corporate rules and generally behave as if they are entitled to do whatever they want to do regardless of how it affects others. Arrogance and vanity accompany them at all stages of their corporate life.

Saneya was our good looking corporate diva with an intellect to match and the apple of the bosses eyes since she was a star performer too.

Archana, Rachita, Anusha, Anand and Subhash were the "friends forever" group that simmered with negativity at all her achievements, "how do I know?" You may ask well yes, not all of us are good at histrionics and their faces would spell out their inner feelings and sentiments. When one is guilty or on guard they tend to draw your attention unknowingly to exactly what they are trying to guard. In this case it was their jealousy and frustration so every time that they made it a point to mention they were very happy at her achievements, in the process they revealed exactly how far removed they were from it in reality.

The advent of the social media has also propagated the self obsessed age with its fair share of selfies, tweeting, instagramming and posting on YouTube and Face Book everything that you do. With all the corporate wisdom that I have amassed in these 25 years plus of experience I would venture a new definition of this trait that manifests itself in certain corporate personalities.

By admonishing, criticizing and saying how difficult such people are to live and work with why don't we tread on the inspirational and positives that this facade has to offer us?

Humbled by the adulation - It's autograph time

It wouldn't be wrong to say that nearly all of us possess one or more narcissistic traits without crossing the line of a diagnosable disorder. I strongly believe and propagate the fact that it is certainly not narcissistic to have a strong sense of self-confidence based on one's abilities.

There are certain professions that give you more opportunities to demonstrate your success and winner status which in turn elicits admiration from others and PR is certainly one of those..

When you encounter such people learn to accept their true competence and potential learn to relate more effectively with them and create a more rewarding relationship. This will not only help you move ahead in life but help you help yourself.

I have seen that as part of a competitive world it is perfectly okay to project your achievements and success. You own that success and therefore have the right and liberty to tell people about it. I take great pride in my achievements and success and that is something which propels me forward to newer and higher ones. The feeling of contentment should never be so strong and pronounced that it envelopes your desire to strive for future achievements and glories.

Unless there is a narcissist in you, your love for self progress and its proclamation will never see the light of day. Go ahead, discover the narcissist in you, crown your glories, love yourself, love whatever you do, talk about it and tell people about your successes because many of them have their face buried in the quicksand of their failures and hardly notice others achievements!

Plant a sapling for them to water and allow to fructify in the process learning how to weed out the plants of jealousy, frustration, dejection, and nurturing the ones that spread the hue of inspiration!

CHAPTER 41

COMPREHENDING THE FINE DIVIDE

Our career offers us a lethal combination of blatant "in the face" messages and the subtle "hope you understand" kind of messages. However, since acceptance and understanding vary with the individuals there are unfortunately numerous misses on this account till there is no option but to substitute the latter with the former and sometimes to a lesser degree the former with the latter.

Samantha was a chirpy teenager when she joined her first job, where she was standing in for the Managing Director's secretary who was on a six month maternity leave. Samantha was a topper and gold medalist from a reputed secretarial school and shorthand institute (before you raise your eyebrows, let me clarify that I am referring to approximately 25 years ago when a qualified secretary then, devoid of the modern day technological aids was well conversant with typing at a high speed and taking dictation in shorthand.)

Her youth and excitement propelled her to enter the imposing austere cabin of the top man of the company without even an iota of fear or apprehension. Her enthusiasm to perform and give her very best was the only predominant feeling that she was enveloped with as she entered the bosses' cabin. She sailed through her first day at work with great ease and had a look of great satisfaction as she wound up for the day. The six months thereafter flew past with Samantha completely ingrained into the corporate system and its way of functioning. The boss was very happy with her performance and when Mrs Patel his previous secretary walked in for once he was at a loss of words and could not find the right ones to tell his Head HR how he wanted Samantha to continue working for him. After a few fumbles and ums and aahs later he did manage to express to his Head HR that although he could not deny Mrs Patel her rightful job, he could contemplate another vacancy in the company. Samanthas' employment was confirmed and she continued to work for the top boss whereas Mrs Patel was transferred to another parallel position within the company.

One fine day when Samantha walked into her cabin she saw a strange and unfamiliar gadget next to her manual typewriter; a few smug looking people walked in a little later and informed her that they had been sent by the IT Head to initiate her to this phenomenal new technological advancement called the computer. Like the animal species who do not welcome strangers in their pack Linda too was very cautious of this monster that would challenge her typing speed and hours of learning and hard work of so many years. The monster of resentment is an alien one and should not be found in the corporate waters, for once it is, it carries along with its flow all who succumb to it into its' hostile and unproductive embrace. Linda unfortunately gave this monster access. Needless to say her work went downhill as she continued adhering to the old school of thought and traditional ways of working.

The advent of technology comes with an inbuilt dictate– you either adopt it or fade away, for no one in the modern scenario can work without it. It touches every employee in some way or the other. Linda tried to ward off its effects on her work by proclaiming that she could work efficiently even without it.

The day of an important meeting dawned and Linda had the bosses presentation ready on an OHP whereas the others presented on power point. The stark difference stood out and was noticed by all present. The boss himself wanted to go a little easy on Linda who was so foolishly headstrong and hoped that good sense would prevail and she would give in to the IT instructors training, but not much changed. She was gradually kept out of the various meetings and all that she would do in the day would be to uncover her manual typewriter and cover it again in the evening. Redundancy started setting in slowly but strongly. Mrs. Patel started walking in and out of the bosses' cabin more frequently and work was delegated to her as before.

Nibbling on her sandwich in the pantry it was her colleague Shashank who finally decided to broach the unbroachable. He gave her a reality shake and told her be ready to adopt new practices if she had to survive in this competitive world. He told her how subtle hints were being dropped, by excluding her from crucial meetings and involving others, giving her less work than the others and sidelining her.

Samantha realized how she had missed the subtle hints and even the "in the face" instances, so blinded was she with her own high opinion of self worth in the face of technology which as she now grudgingly admitted was a little misplaced.

Chucking the half eaten sandwich into the dustbin, she hurried to the IT Head's cabin displaying the same enthusiasm and excitement with which she had walked in a few years ago ready to take on the corporate world, except this time a few years later, it was to blend the world of technology into her existing corporate world to create success!

The fine line between redundancy and employability blurs with the passage of years, but a constant process of reinvention strengthens the demarcation and creates a distinct division.

CHAPTER 42

CELEBRATION AND ALIENATION

In a goal oriented work culture, we have ample opportunities to celebrate success. An organization that cares for the successes of its employees to give it due importance and celebrate it, also creates a healthy and positive work environment. One of the German Multinationals I worked for was very keen to celebrate every little employee achievement and the HR & PR department worked in close harmony to encourage and reward employees. While this created an atmosphere of goodwill and encouragement in the benefactors it created a feeling of healthy competition in a certain group of employees, it bred resentment and alienation in another.

The Finance department was always a fore runner of all that was good and positive. It had the most hardworking and sincere employees who worked hard and produced the most enviable balance sheets. They carried out the paperless office syndrome to the t and soft copies were the "in thing" with information at the click of a button. My personal observation is that success and celebrations start pushing you higher till you start looking down and finally losing sight of the ones still lurking below. I for one celebrate every small success of mine because it motivates me to outperform myself. It releases happy hormones in my system and keeps me work healthy and smiling. I am of the opinion that although success can be had and enjoyed unlimited without a cap on it, it is for the others to absorb it in moderation without getting negatively affected. I have also observed that although celebration follows success alienation is self devised. Nathan loudly applauded the achievements of the Finance department but silently simmered at his own inability to get rewarded for anything that he did. It was so easy to read though his disgruntled look and gauge his resentment.

So restless was he and so desperate to catch others on a wrong foot that he gradually started distancing himself from the other employees, taking his James Bond and Sherlock Holmes role too seriously, he started eyeing each and every activity of his colleagues as something that could be reported to the higher ups as going against company policies. His relentless pursuit in the cat and mouse game eventually saw some movement when one day he noticed Ravi from the Finance department speaking in whispers to his colleague Kant. The moment they saw Nathan, they immediately became silent waiting for him to pass by before resuming their conversation. This was the trigger and opportunity that he had been waiting for. The whole day was an action packed day for him when he started tracing their suspicious (according to him) activity. He noted down the number of hours they spent after office thus wasting electricity, the number of cups of tea coffee the entire department had, the expenditure on snacks dinner etc (all he had to do was to lurk around after office hours and just follow the office boy whenever he went outside to order food and later go up to the restaurant to ask how much the bill was for saying he was from the same company and had come to pay but unfortunately arrived later than the office boy.)

Nathan made his way home in the wee hours of the morning consumed with excitement at the discovery of misuse of office funds on electricity, fuel (as company cars had been plying back and forth) and the private in cabin dining of the Finance department. He had it all in hand, bills, notes et all. After swiping in for work and sitting at his desk for an hour he thought he would walk into the MDs cabin a feat he had only been dreaming off till date and announce in a bold voice how he had been observing the trespasses of the Finance team. Before he could as much as get up though, he noticed a flurry of activities, burly men and two women walking inside the office, asking everyone to switch off their cell phones and locking the door from inside to prevent anybody from exiting or entering the office. It was then that the unpleasant realization dawned on Nathan – this was indeed an Income Tax raid.

After a full day of grilling key employees, going through records it was time for the officials to leave. The high charged action drama that had started in the morning and unfolded during the day concluded with a happy ending as they recorded their satisfaction at the maintenance of company records and bid all the employees goodbye permitting us to leave office.

The Finance team had the day before come to know of these surprise raids being conducted at different companies and had in fact geared up to pre empt this in case our company was on their list. They had worked hard to keep all their records clear and accessible (not that they had manipulated or done anything out of the way because this company was very fair in its practices and was an acclaimed ethical corporate citizen.) They had made numerous trips to the factory go down (that explained the various trips of the office cars) to pull out the previous year's files and stack them all in one place so that in case the IT department chose to visit our office all the files would be at one place without last minute unnecessary trips to the godown and this is exactly what happened otherwise this entire process would have taken more than a day with employees locked up inside the office for longer. The Finance department had made extra efforts through their foresight and quick action to ensure that the inconvenience caused to one and all was minimal. They had in fact put their personal convenience and work timings at stake to accommodate the convenience of others.

A day later, the company organized a snack event in the conference room with tea / coffee / soft drinks being served resounding to the sounds of applause as the Finance team was celebrated yet again for its immaculate work execution. There were a pair of hands though that were not a part of the applauding team for they were busy tearing up documents that had been so meticulously gathered to show that particular department in poor light. Yes, it was Nathan with his eyes set on the dustbin making use of his hands for a different totally avoidable and baseless task.

Whereas celebrations around success are inevitable, we are the procreators of alienation by allowing it to affect us negatively!

CHAPTER 43

KNOTS AND CROSSES

Enrichment, disillusionment, setbacks, positive and negative experiences are the hallmarks of any career. When you are a couple of years into your professional life you gain the supremacy or crown of an evaluator. You are in a position from where you can either look back or look down upon (depending on your vantage point) on all that has transpired during the years. Each experience, each emotion, each step contributing its bit either to the safe deposit vault of your career or to the garbage bins outside.

When Nitu and Shravan started their career as freshers and interns in a company of their choice, they never for once imagined that their initial dislike and animosity for each other would translate into a knot for life. Days at work and days outside the office all stem from what lies within us to eventually give it shape and form.

Going back to my days as a newbie I recall the various instances when whatever I did however hard I tried I could not please my superiors or my colleagues. This did not occur due to my lack of initiative or performance but just because their expectations were different and my view point did not match theirs. I gradually learnt the art of crossing out the negative in the outcome and sieving the wheat from the chaff by highlighting whatever good had emerged out of it and taking it as a learning experience for the next attempt.

I can also recall instances when I did outstanding work and surprised the team members and won their goodwill, trust, and affection. This was the knot of team spirit and unity that saw me through many a corporate storms and turbulences.

The topography of corporate life is dotted with valleys, hills, plateaus watered by the perennial stream of human emotions and experiences. As you place yourself in a little boat rowing it towards your goal, rapids, meanders and various obstacles may come in your way compelling you to change direction. You may have to adapt, and change course since that would probably be the need of the hour but one must never lose sight of the goal.

Drawing inspiration from a jewellery store, we must scan through all that is on display, yet settle only for precious and semi precious stones which we can afford to strew our corporate path with. This retention of the good and dismissal of the negative is not limited to experiences only; it stretches beyond that to relationships.

The word relationship itself is so inspiring that one is tempted to use it to one's advantage and work on those, networking to our heart's content.

The takeaways from any career are the tangible and intangible advantages which we term knots and are the reason for the strong bonds of love, trust and togetherness between colleagues and business associates. The disheartening and unpleasant experiences can well be slotted under crosses and erased from our memory and future action plan.

We are the designers and creators of the knots and crosses of the fabric of our corporate life!

CHAPTER 44

MUCH ADO ABOUT LOVE IS NEEDED

One of the most oft used but most confusing words is Love. It can evoke your passionate best or make you wallow in the nadir of emotions when you refer to this. Love for our career is not something instantaneous and rarely "love at first sight." For me, my career started with a thought which in turn generated emotions of excitement, anticipation and a host of other emotions which at that point of time lay latent and undiscovered.

I have during the course of my career met several people who mouth the same "I love my job line." My corporate interactions however revealed many facets of love. Anna D'Souza was brimming with this emotion she called love every day that she came to work. She would be her chirpy best and well dressed ready to take on the routine as well as the new challenges that her work unfolded each day and I realized that since Anna was social and extrovert the aspect that appealed the most to her in her job as the Hospitality Manager was her interaction with people and people management. She was adept at handling various situations which her job demanded and loved using her skills at that. Probing a little further one could see that she was more in love with the outcome of her actions and her success than the challenge of the task itself.

Seema, on the other hand was in love with technology since her job as the overseas project coordinator demanded the use of the latest developments in technology, her love for her job was a great learning opportunity and perpetual voyage of discovery with the adaptation of new technology.

Shyman Sundar was in an unhappy marriage with a family of 5 to take care of, time at home was far from pleasant. An apt summary and the highlights of his family life would be - a few hours of sleep, between arguments and anger tantrums, frayed tempers, high decibel levels, and the daunting task of making corners meet after supporting the incessant demands of his wife and children. He loved his work because it provided a much needed getaway from this stifling atmosphere as he could spend 8 hours of peace, well work pressures were better than the peacelessness that his marital life offered him every day on his return home.

Vidyawati was the perfect embodiment of pure unadulterated love for her job. She was in love with her profession and everything that it brought with it. She could talk animatedly about the intricacies of her software development job, research and keep abreast with the latest that the field had to offer and never ever feel dejected at any of her failures. She would in fact look at ways and means to improve her performance every day.

I too was not far removed from the love that Vidyawati felt for her profession. I can recall my all consuming passion for my profession coupled with my initial trepidation, hesitation to try out new ideas. Then the strength of my desire ensured that I did away with all negativity and perform according to my ideas and plans. A few roadblocks and small failures made me despise it only to start loving it again after a while. The see saw of love and hate in any career is an occupational hazard.

Every professional loves their work, and mouthing the 3 words – "I love you" is more of a fad than an expression of your emotions. It is time that we stepped back and analysed what makes us love our work and try and energize the reason periodically!

CHAPTER 45

EMBRACING YOUR INNER SELF

Sheetal, walked out of the office staring intently at her cell phone. It was old and outdated as most of the things she had at home. Her meagre salary did not allow her luxuries. Starting off the next day for her periodic visits to suppliers, she noticed how many times she had to switch off and switch on her phone since the number of years it had served her and its overusage would make it stall occasionally.

She whizzed past all her client visits and compiled her report ready to be presented to the Management the other day. A beaming Mrs. Joshi her mother opened the door and congratulated her. It took a few minutes for Sheetal to ask her the reason for the greeting, but without saying a word she handed over a gift wrapped box to her. The scrawl on the card read "Thank you for being such a wonderful and sincere worker."

Still befuddled at this mystery gift, Sheetal proceeded to unwrap it and a few layers later she could see the beautiful champagne gold colour of the latest I phone peeping at her from inside. "Ma who gave this to you?" but her question met with another smile from her mother who said that it was hand delivered by someone who said he was from the office. There wasn't too much of a guessing game needed because no sooner had she asked her mom about the gift, a loud message beep shook her out of her daze. The one line text to her made it amply clear who the sender was. Kamal was the second generation management by virtue of being the Chairman's son of a company that supplied raw material to her corporate. Kamal being the restless, nouveau riche was impatient and wanted things to move at a fast pace. The new cell phone was his way of encouraging Sheetal to recommend his company over others. An infuriated Sheetal told her mother that there was a stark difference between a gift and bribe and this most certainly fell into the latter.

Mrs. Joshi was a woman of the world who had seen a lot of hardships devoid of sparks of generosity and liberalities that gifts and surprises brought along with them. She therefore evaluated this gesture in a different light and tried to reason out with Sheetal that this was not cash that was being given, it was just as if somebody would send across something on her birthday. It soon dawned on her though, that in her bid to coax Sheetal into acceptance she herself could see all that was wrong with the gift. It is true when they say that your inner self is the truthful unpretentious self and this was one such occasion when it emerged in all its brilliance to beckon the office boy to Sheetal's home and ensure the safe passage of this gift from her hands to the client's with a note which spelt her disapproval at this gesture.

When you are at a responsible position in your career and at a comfortable height, you are prone to being shaken out of your comfort zone where you may not have many faces to turn to for counseling. You do find yourself as the sole decision maker many a times. It is at these times that you take recourse to your inner self and churn out the right from the wrong, the wise from the foolish and impulsive.

Come April, May, June and you are in thick of reviewing your juniors progress and either handing out the standard annual increment or rewarding them with better increments and raises. Kamal was a hard working, sincere affable boy and got along well with everyone in the organization. Ritu was the more reserved and quiet types who had to be cajoled into striking a conversation or opening her mouth in meetings. Ritu was Kamal's junior and always under his protective umbrella, she would rarely be heard voicing anything on her own, everything that she said or did within the office space would be routed through Kamal.

The whole office was gearing up to the end of the financial year and keeping their records and files in order and implicitly also trying to create a good impression for their impending appraisals. Kamal moved around with an air of authority doing his bit and also instructing all in his department to do so.

The remaining months passed and it was indeed the most looked forward to time of the year- appraisal time! The routine appraisals took place and I reviewed the seniors and signed the dotted line for their incentives and raises. The one review where I faltered was Kamal's. His presentation was perfect, his documents were in order and there was nothing apparently wrong with his performance, yet I could not convince myself to giving him a liberal increment. There was an uneasiness that set in and my inner self told me to re assess his performance.

It was one of those rare evenings when I was leaving much later than the office closing hours, because as a practice I abhor late hours and live by the saying that one has to work smarter and stretch our office timings only in case of dire emergency. I also believe in the mobile office concept where I am accessible 24 x7 and which is not restricted to my geographical location alone. In fact, I can be at work wherever I am, if I deem it important. The dim light in the cabin attracted my attention and I walked closer to see who it was. A few steps closer and I could see Kamal's silhouette. He was talking to somebody, a woman, yes Ritu. I could have walked past since there was nothing unusual about a boss talking to his subordinate and giving instructions, yet there was something sinister in the whole conversation. I could hear a visibly agitated Kamal and a sobbing Ritu saying "No Sir this is wrong."

With so much awareness and talk on sexual harassment at the workplace I grit my teeth and was wondering if it was something along those angles which I would have to resolve when I flung the door open. I was about to push the door open when I heard what the conversation was about. It was thankfully not what I had imagined it would be but it was Kamal trying to yank a file from Ritu's hands which she was resisting. I was so close to discovering the cause yet so far away if I continued standing outside that I decided to throw open the doors and announce my entry. Both of them were taken aback as I demanded an explanation of what was transpiring. Kamal kept gasping for breath unable to speak, but it was Ritu who sprang up and told me that Kamal had gathered a lot of our confidential company information in the file which she was holding on to and was going to hand it over to our competitor. They had apparently offered him a job and he was just waiting to get his annual increment letter so that he could bargain with them for a higher package. This information was an added advantage that he would take with him to increase his worth.

Now I understood what my inner self was trying to tell me my conscience was telling me that Kamal was not worthy of either my trust or the company's.

The appraisal letters were handed out by me a couple of days later except that the roles were reversed when it came to Kamal, he handed me a letter instead of me doing so. Yes, it was his resignation letter . As for Ritu; she was promoted and took Kamal's position.

Our Inner self is our true self – untouched by the grime and pollution of the outside world. Listen to it and rely on its brilliance to guide you through the dull and dark moments of your career !

CHAPTER 46

LEADERS AND QUITTERS

A well grounded observation would be that with a career you also enter a high risk zone and volatile territory in many ways.

You can at best choose your profession, your department, your company, your geographical location but one eminent risk is you cannot choose either your colleagues or your boss. While you can diminish the former's impact by the wide choice that it brings, you inherit the latter and have zero control over that situation.

Suryakant was a highly motivated and enthusiastic employee; he literally breezed in to work on his first day, had a spring in his step and was looking forward to his new job. Mr. Ramanathan his boss and HOD had served the company for 20 years and defined all that was old school and cautious. He was averse to taking any risks or going against the accepted, tried and tested norms. He secretly believed that his number of years in this job were a result of this cautious approach of treading the trodden path and not swerving from that ever. All the members of his department were by now used to his non experimental, dull and mundane style of working as a result of which, they never attempted any innovative ideas, or a different approach to work. This department would have been an apt example of a typical 9 to 5 job where you clocked in, did your work diligently and left at the prescribed time.

Creativity, innovation, excitement and enthusiasm were alien words for the members of this department. A few years into his job and the spring in Suryakant's step went missing. His enthusiasm was replaced by a routine existence in a 9 to 5 time frame.

Mr. Irani was one of those bosses who was more like a pal and one had to struggle to get the word Sir out in a formal gathering or meeting. Extreme empowerment, trust and great liberty to experiment in one's job was what Irani believed in. He would be happier if you experimented, attempted and failed rather than not attempting and implementing new ideas. His department was characterized with a new thrill everyday, where employees were challenged to think of new ideas and implement best practices at work. Team spirit and employee bonding were at an all time high in this department. He gave a lot of encouragement to employee growth and motivation. The working hours here were dominated more by the upbeat mood and need of the employee than by the rules of punctuality and attendance.

As for me, a blend of good luck and good work dominated my corporate sojourn. I was lucky to have had bosses who encouraged me in furthering my self growth and development. When my first boss noticed that I had the potential to be a good employee he not only gave me great empowerment at work to not only carry it in a manner that I deemed effective but also promoted my physical and mental stimulation by sanctioning corporate memberships for golf and reading clubs after office hours. They were the stimulators for employee success and company growth. I continued to do well in my job spurred and motivated by the support and encouragement coming my way. As I progressed in my work and underwent company shifts, the bosses that came as a part of the change gave me no reason to complain. In fact with the modern surge of the age bracket of the Senior Management going lower, I was at one time reporting to a boss who was more than 20 years my junior. It was almost as if God understood my preference for good grooming and good looks as he handpicked the best for me. I may be inviting a lot of flak when I say that although I take great pride in the fact that I am a dedicated and sincere employee, we know that congenial conditions at work enhance performance. As for me, I work best in handsome, intellectually capable, smart and well attired male boss conditions.

I have never had the opportunity to have a female boss but do hope that some of my juniors whom I lead as a boss would echo the same sentiments that I do, above.

While so much has been said about bosses and their style of working where they can be old school, new school, liberal, denying novelty and experimentation or just apathetic to you, we must not forget that this is a high risk zone with differently abled employees and receptive or apathetic bosses.

Karan was on the lookout for any opportunity where he could promote his secretary Pervez beyond work related aspects. He sanctioned her enrollment for local language classes to enhance her fluency in the local language and also for her to get an opportunity to learn something new, he sanctioned her golf membership, a corporate club membership where she could socialize after office hours, but Pervez was the unassuming, unambitious types. She was most comfortable stretching out on a sofa at home watching TV after office hours. All the perks went unacknowledged and unutilized by her. It was the proverbial case of "You can lead a horse to water but can't make it drink."

Bosses are an unspoken legacy of the corporate culture. They can either give you wings, or clip them. They can either make you dependant and robotic in your performance or they can give you the freedom to operate and the liberty to use your discretion in doing so.

Good leaders create more leaders and increase their tribe whereas poor ones create a culture of quitters and deplete their circle of employees!

CHAPTER 47

THE NATIONAL IN THE INTERNATIONAL

With the world becoming a global village, for most employees travel is strongly intertwined with their work engagement. There are overseas trainings, meetings, customer visits and so on which an employee must engage in at one point of time or the other in his career.

Meena came from a small village in Maharashtra, and moving out of there into a city was in itself a tremendous decision for her and her family, so when her name was proposed for a six month training in New York she was paranoid with trepidation and fear. The sight of an aeroplane flying high in the sky was a good viewing experience for her but to imagine herself in it was petrifying. As part of the Exports Department of the company she was assigned an important task wherein she had to travel to the parent company in New York and take training on various job related issues. This announcement struck her like a bolt of lightning and her stable corporate world received a big jolt with this strong tremor. Then there were the aftershocks of her misgivings regarding clothing, food and so on where she was at her wits end and even contemplated quitting the job for the sake of preserving her untainted nationality. What bothered her most was the thought of the reactions of her family and contacts in her native town. Venturing out of the confines of the small village to the modern city where she was working now all alone contributed to their gossip for many months but how would they react if they came to know about this across the seven seas trip?

As I was getting ready to step into my car and leave for the day I saw a hesitant Meena walk up towards me mouthing a very low "Mam I want to speak to you." I asked her what was bothering her and it was then that I learnt about her travel apprehensions. Deciding that this was neither the time nor the place to address this daunting concern, I asked her to meet me the next day and meanwhile to sleep over this.

Rialto Bridge in the City of love and Romance - Venice - Italy

The next day brought her to my cabin, nothing much had changed, and it was the same fears and apprehensions that were voiced the previous day. I started off by addressing this in a mentally structured way. I made her see the positivity in her career and this choice; I even played on the woman angle, and yes, why not? There were 5 men in her department, two of them senior to her, but by sheer dint of hard work and merit she had jumped the queue. The face is a wonderful mirror and it takes great skill and practice to conceal your inner feelings. Meena was unfortunately a novice at that and I could see that I had created a great beginning. The rest of the conversation was smooth sailing. I gave her some valuable tips on how she could adapt to the culture shock and the first time flying experience, because at the end of it she would emerge a wiser and well travelled person, a tag that most of the employees in the office would like to wear on their shoulders. I could sense a clean sweep but was waiting for official confirmation as she walked out of my cabin with a pensive look on her face.

Yes, I did it! She came back after an hour with a confident "Yes mam I will travel!" After landing at New York, the first call that she made was to me. Gone was the timidity in her voice. It was replaced by an excitement that was ready to take on the world. Encouragement for her was in order, which I lavished in full measure. I realized that one thing that keeps you going in foreign lands is your communication with a few chosen and close few in your country of residence. A routine call to me and her family became the order of the day and contributed in a large measure to her increasing self confidence in a hitherto alien land.

Time they say flies very fast and here too 6 months passed very soon. It was time for Meena to return.

I actually did what I had only thought of doing in a good number of years at work – that of playing the recording of the security camera installed on my cabin door entrance. The recording of six months earlier showed Meena with a distinct falter in her steps, hesitation in opening her mouth and frowns and lines of worry on her good looking face and compared it with the latest one which spelt confidence with a capital C.

Inspiration from the oldest bookstore in the world - Bertrand Chiado
Bookstore in Lisbon, Portugal

Recounting her various International exploits, she mentioned how she had geared up to the flavours of their food and mixed and matched it to her Indianness. How she continued wearing the traditional outfits with a twist of the western and which became a great craze for the locals who asked her to demonstrate how to wear the wonderful combo of clothes. She had also made a couple of good and interesting friends outside work with whom she could socialize.

She suddenly grew very animated while mentioning all the learning that she had amassed from her work, and how she was confident of imparting her new found knowledge to the others for an enhanced working system of the organization.

With a smile on my face when I asked her to tell me her take away from the experience this is what she said –

"You don't have to lose your individuality or Indianness to merge with the foreign cultures, at best what is needed is an open mind to adapt and function productively because people out there are also receptive with open minds and they absorb and accept you easily!"

Resisting the strong urge to applaud I shook hands with the new Meena. I kept my little secret of the comparison of the previous and current recordings burying it under my smile as I bid adieu to her. Her personality had undergone an immense sea change. The confident, well spoken lady who walked in briskly today was indeed The Indian who was New York returned!

The unique characteristics that we possess are inherent to our environment and country, by attempting to blur that divide and gradually diminish it is no measure of acceptability and success in another!

CHAPTER 48

THE ART IN THE CRAFT

I have often come across an oft asked question, is there any art in every profession or is it limited to only the artists? Picture this; most of us would like to proclaim that we have been creative and innovative at work, so if we do that where does the creativity come from? Is it correlated to our inner creativity, lovingly mothered and raised by Art? All of us feel the stirring of creativity at some point or the other of our career, some of us feel it more often than the others. This creativity brings out the artist in us where it animates our style of being and a career filled with the desire to innovate, explore and transform our dreams to reality at work.

A brisk walk through Hyde Park is one of the most looked forward to physical activity when I have work in London. I prefer this to the cushioned luxurious interiors of the hotel gymnasium. On one such occasion in biting cold weather with a light drizzle I made up my mind to brave the outdoors and invigorate my spirits. To say that it was an easy task would be far removed from what it was actually but I was pleasantly surprised to see many like minded people who valued the clean fresh air walking along with me. Wee hours in the morning and my mind a blank slate not yet pondering on the numerous messages and emails that I had received from India. I was determined to give this physical activity my entire dedication devoid of any mental turmoil.

Pausing to rest on a bench which was tucked away in a corner my active mind and eyes took in all that nature had to offer. As my view spanned to the left I noticed an ice cream cart and a very noisy group of 4 children around it. The woman with them was obviously having a difficult time controlling them, I did not even for a moment reflect on whether they were her children or if she was just a friendly neighbourhood aunt or nanny entrusted with this task of walking the kids through Hyde Park. Her body language gave me some indication of the cause of the argument and the volley of cries that ensued (because they were not within ear shot) confirmed my suspicion. I gathered that they were all asking for an ice cream and she was dissuading them to do so. The reason could be any – the cold weather, lack of pounds but whatever it was she was not making any headway and the screaming and shouting continued unabated, in fact worsening and growing louder with the passage of time.

It was then that I noticed her pointing to something – yes I then caught sight of a few pretty ducks in the pond in the centre with some bird feed kept on the side. Excitedly, 3 of the children ran towards the ducks with curiosity and were entrusted with the wonderful task of feeding them. The one that stayed back was unconvinced and continued screaming his lungs out. With 3 small bundles of mischief out of her way, she looked at the little one who still stood his ground, then she rummaged in her purse for change, and handed it over to the ice cream seller in exchange for an ice cream for the sobbing boy. The cold weather was uncongenial to melting the ice cream and the boy was running out of patience only after a few licks. At the same time he could not look away from his other 3 friends who were having a whale of a time at the pond. He started feeling alienated and lonely and the pond was suddenly more inviting than the ice cream but he continued standing his ground and finished the ice cream, thus providing a more orderly and quieter spectacle.

What happened to me then was something very dramatic it was a flash of insight, a bright spark of resolution to a long standing office problem and a little inner voice that whispered to me "yes, go ahead and try it, it will work."

I always took great pride in my leadership and good communication skills but of late as the M.D of my company I had been questioning those, as the HR department was making news for all the wrong reasons. There was a coterie of 4 (with 1 being the ringleader and boss under whose instructions they functioned,) who were always rubbing shoulders the wrong way with their colleagues and there were a lot of complaints against them. I tried to counsel them on many occasions and was even a little tough with them but to no avail. I now knew how to deal with the situation, I would transfer 3 of them to the administration department since they had skill sets to match and give the ring leader a completely new team to lead. Hopefully the 3 sans the 4th would function well and the 4th just to save face would continue standing his ground and taking charge of his existing department.

I continued my walk with a smile on my face I had actually walked on my problem instead of sleeping on it.

Back in office a snack party was in order to celebrate the interdepartmental transfer and I made sure to have ice cream on the menu!

There is an art in every craft and your inner self holds the key, you just need to be receptive, so that you discover and master it!

CHAPTER 49

STAYING AFLOAT

When you set your foot on the treadmill of your career, you should be prepared to encounter different speed and energy levels and match your pace accordingly. The heady pace of a new job, a new career along with its apprehensions and excitement keeps you energized and enthused. The satisfaction that I had, just looking at my first appointment letter is unparalleled till date. My eyes just took in the appointment date from --------- and did not get deterred by the paltry sum mentioned as my remuneration. Preparing for my day at work, clothes, tiffin, etc became the order of the day and the routine chores excited me no end. As I inched my way up and then literally took a steep climb, the all consuming thought mid career was how to stay afloat.

The mid career crisis leaves you with a helpless "I am too young to retire and too old to easily find another job at a commensurate level kind of feeling." When the 50 year old Johnson walked into a National Conference that was open only to Senior Managers and above, he walked in just in time and just before the conference started to an already filled hall, all he could see was young and younger people, in fact he was probably the oldest one in the gathering. During the earlier days, and even when I was coming up the ranks of corporate life, companies required at least 10 years of experience to qualify for mid-manager positions. As we approached that requirement in my early 40s, a shift happened, and we were suddenly over-qualified for those same positions. "Over-qualified" was the new code for "too old," as companies looked at hiring younger talent because they were perceived to have better working knowledge of technology and were employable at lower salary levels.

As a result of this shift the 40 + people including me started feeling threatened and were engulfed with the all consuming passion of how to stay afloat in the corporate world and chosen career. This shift had a trickledown effect on my perception as well. My earlier presumptions of how age was not a merit for promotion or a spring board for the corporate ladder, made me pause and reflect on this presumption in the wake of the new developments in the corporate world.

The 40+ plus felt that the younger candidates did not have adequate business sense and while they could execute the job based on their knowledge they lacked the wisdom and experience that should accompany it. The younger candidates however felt that the older ones while having enough work experience lacked the knowledge of new technology and modern developments.

Johnson and I both felt the need to stay afloat and not sink in the modern world of career requirements, so we got together and discussed our next course of action.

The starting point of our deliberations was our common insatiable appetite and curiosity to learn new things, and adapt those learnings into our work life. This made us head towards the private computer coaching classes, not bothering about how it impacted our finances and after office hour's family life.

A good two months of "hands on" experience and armed with new learning, we made a more confident entry into the office. We could participate more at conferences, meetings and routine work and were more readily welcomed and accepted with our new found confidence.

We learnt that while things still work in established and time tested ways, our career gives us great room for experimenting and discovering how to improve things. New solutions can replace the old ones without harming the outcome, but expediting the process in a tech savvy way.

We noted that adapting to new business practices is not just a fad but the need of the hour. One of the major tricks of staying afloat is not to hold on to or remain steadfast to traditional business practices, and those who commit the mistake of doing so are on an exponentially quickening timeline to extinction. In fact a completely new business mindset is needed.

While Johnson and I discovered the new business mantra Julie having served 25 years in the company refused to give way to the new model of working, she would insist on the old way of communicating with employees on typed inter office memos with signature acknowledgements, making the tasks time drawn lengthy and using avoidable man power.

So firmly entrenched was she in her comfort zone that she would not allow even a chink in her time tested work armour. She gradually alienated herself from the other employees as she would never seek their opinion or try and incorporate new methods and learning. She gradually drifted out as deadwood and with the burden of her unbudging stance sank into oblivion soon.

The million dollar truth that dawned on me was that the aging out of the workplace is not related to the number of years that you have spent at work or how old you are, it is ironically related to how outdated your mindset is and how rigid you are in your stance and resolve not to change.

Companies need to evolve and change with new business practices and technology and most importantly the demand of the business, those who are receptive to change will be the best positioned for future growth. The employees too must do that.

There is much wisdom in the saying "The Old Order Changeth yielding place to new" and we must realise that what was once new soon becomes old, you can stay afloat in your career only when you can cling on to the lifebuoy of adaptation!

CHAPTER 50

THE ETERNAL BOND

The word eternal was never so poignant and meaningful as it is today, at this stage of my career. It is suffused with a world of meaning and experience for me. I ventured, I tried, I tested, I failed on a few occasions, sprang back to my feet again, never letting my buoyancy feel the weight of occasional failures, or criticism that was liberally strewed by passersby. It was almost as if I clung on to my belief of making my choice work. In the wilderness of suitors and choices when your eyes rest on a tiny spark you fuel it with your passion and resolve to make it brighter. It is that spark that lights your path as you move along, it's that glow that makes you see the right from the wrong, it is that brilliance that prevents you from tripping on the treacherous and rocky patches that come along with the landscape.

When our young steps lose their sprightliness and agility, this is the torch that guides them through. Our heavier older steps do not falter but plod continuously and steadily because it is this beacon of our hope and aspirations that illuminates our road. When we set out on our path we have our inner resources and strength packed and ready to be unwrapped as and when needed. We just have to pull them out and use them judiciously to our advantage to navigate the minefield of our career.

It would not be wrong to say that a similarity in answers would emerge if you were to ask people what gave them the most dissatisfaction, the high rankers undoubtedly would be love and career. These are incredibly important pillars of your waking life. When you walk into your career you realize that it is not what rom coms had portrayed it to be, it is in fact more complex and evolving with a myriad hues lending their shades to colour it at different junctures. I evolved a pragmatic approach of looking at my career as my partner, the one that I was committed to for life. There are occasions when we celebrate our togetherness, there are occasions when I question my choice and compare it with others, but it's what I come back to every day. It's there to stay. I have seen it, known it and understood it in all its facets, I have admired it and applauded it for all the joys it has and can give me. I have even felt stirrings of envy when I have seen another talking lovingly about it or with a greater degree of animation than I ever did. These are the times when I have realized the need to give myself a shot in the arm, a booster that was needed to revive my longing and love for it.

It has now become so integral and ingrained in my being that my career is my romance, my passion, my love. The initial misgivings and doubts have all been blown away by the strong gust of love and passion. The passage of years has in fact fanned the spark that was ignited years ago, and today I am poised at my receptive best where I can still feel the butterflies ballad in my belly, still feel like a lost teenager in the presence of that special someone. I am confident as I reassure myself that this is indeed the mystical piece that completes the puzzle of my professional life, lends coherence to the occasional anarchy. This is indeed the special love that has swept me off my feet. It is this charm, this spell that entwines me with it in a "forever and ever" fairy tale of romance, as my career and I continue our walk together on the magical path ahead unwavering, with great resolve, grit, determination and happiness never to falter never to stumble, united with a common purpose and a common mission **"till death do us part !"**

EPILOGUE

The all pervading emotion of my career has, is and will always be Love. This is not limited to the mushiness of love which includes teary eyed girls, boys, men and women; this is in fact that emotion, the strength that any professional dips into at the start of his work life. Love is in fact what makes an individual's career go around.

As for my love story, I have traced it all in **"Romancing your Career"** right from the time when I felt its first stirrings, in the idea, the thought of a career itself, I have experienced both its highs and lows with the same intensity, whether it was to rejoice in the former or to learn from the latter. It has been a passionate, unbridled and incessant journey so far. Love is the reason that makes me jump into bed each night so that I can be ready and fresh for the multiple opportunities that my work unfolds before me day after day and love is the reason for me to jump out of bed to welcome those, and relish them and adorn my professional world with.

I have witnessed such a wide gamut of emotions during my rich and diverse work tenure that I feel enriched and empowered. This very empowerment saw my entrepreneurial streak shaping up in 2005, as I named my company, quite obviously **"Empowered Solutions."** My enthusiasm for my profession continues unabated, the passage of years spurring me on with a "Never Say Die" spirit. This is one romance which will never see "a happily ever after "ending. This is one story that has no ending, for love is ageless, love is timeless and it will continue its saga in every professional who loves his or her career.

My secret pact with my suitor – My last breath in his warm embrace with my stilletoes on, still active, still working!

Challenge Your Limits - Aim High!

First Indian speaker to address PRSSA SFO, USA (2012)

Winner of the Highest National Award in PR (2012)

The Indian Achievers Award - 2017

www.ingramcontent.com/pod-product-compliance
Lightning Source LLC
Chambersburg PA
CBHW030006190526
45157CB00014B/710